T0146395

THE PRESENT.

A MINDFULNESS HANDBOOK FOR THE EVERYDAY GURU

JASON PAUL JELICICH

BALBOA.PRESS
A DIVISION OF HAY HOUSE

Balboa Press books may be ordered through booksellers or by contacting:

Balboa Press
A Division of Hay House
1663 Liberty Drive
Bloomington, IN 47403
www.balboapress.com.au
AU TFN: 1 800 844 925 (Toll Free inside Australia)
AU Local: (02) 8310 7086 (+61 2 8310 7086 from outside Australia)

Print information available on the last page.

ISBN: 978-1-5043-0507-5 (sc)
ISBN: 978-1-5043-0508-2 (e)

Balboa Press rev. date: 11/15/2022

This is The Present.

Welcome.

Warning:

The contents of this book may cause you to think.
If this happens to you, please take a deep breath and exhale slowly.
Hopefully, it won't last long.

For Tyson, Hunter, Cormac & Elodie

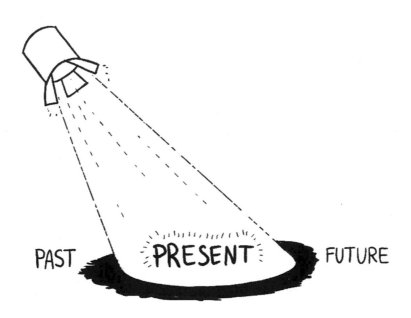

PAST   PRESENT   FUTURE

'Our deepest fear is not that we are inadequate.
Our deepest fear is that we are powerful beyond measure.
It is our light, not our darkness, that most frightens us.'
~ Marianne Williamson

Table of Contents

Foreword.

It gives me great joy to write the foreword for this wonderful book.

When it comes to improving our own quality of life, there are few more powerful things we can do than to be focused in the present moment; that's why this book is so important for our time. In a world that is getting ever faster and increasingly busy, we can lose ourselves in the traumatic experiences of the past or the anxieties of the future. This book, however, will help bring you back to what's truly important in life and to live from the only time that truly exists – the present moment.

With his background in hospitality, Jason has interacted with all types of individuals and groups, giving him unique insights on the commonality and universality of where we can get off track and unknowingly sabotage our own happiness. Combining this with his high-level credentials as a motivational speaker and self-development expert, as well as a personal passion to help others, he is the perfect person to write this book.

Perhaps, what I most like about this book is the way it is structured in practical, bite-sized nuggets of wisdom that can be easily digested and implemented anywhere, anytime. It has not been written from some hard to grasp 'mystical' standpoint, but from a real-world, put-it-to-work-now kind of way, making it accessible to the most pragmatic of us.

I believe this book represents a great gift, or 'present', that you can give to yourself – and to others – each day. I congratulate Jason on putting it together in such a beautiful, practical and concise way that may help many millions enjoy a healthier, happier life by learning to get back to, and enjoy, the present more and more.

I'm sure you will get what you need from this book, as I'm sure Jason did in putting it together for you.

Yours in great health,

Mark Bunn – International Health Speaker and Bestselling author of *Ancient Wisdom for Modern Health*

Acknowledgments.

Everyone supposedly has a 'book inside them', but it sometimes takes a small army of people to yank it out of us and turn it into something tangible.

The genesis of this book, and in fact, much of my interest in this subject, began with a book my mother gave me many moons ago, *Be Here Now* by Baba Ram Dass. His talks, writings and - even well into his 80s - his twitter feed, have helped me keep in touch with most important thing that I can control over in this world: my own state of being.

For as long as I can remember, my mother has piped these sorts of books through to me – perhaps sensing that I needed all the help I could get! Her personal inscriptions penned in books such Richard Bach's *Illusions*, Kahlil Gibran's *The Prophet*, Eckhart Tolle's *The Power of Now* and *A New Earth*, echo both her own interests and her loving support of my own evolution. Thanks, Mum.

My father also provided interest and encouragement here, sending me Ram Dass cassette tapes and transcripts of his talks, as well as introducing me to Eric Fromm's *To Have or to Be* and Aldous Huxley's *The Doors of Perception*. While long separated, and with vastly different lifestyles, my parents came together around the notion that *being* is more important than *having*, and both are represented in the pages and intent of this book.

Then there's my editor, Kris Albertson, who had the unenviable task of taking my random collection of ideas and awkward grammar, and guiding it to towards a finished product. Thanks for suffering through those first drafts and being available for a Skype chat at the wrong end of your own time zone. Without your practical and insightful contributions, I would not be writing this section today.

The many illustrations are also an integral part of this book; I had the idea very early on to include simple line drawings that would capture and illuminate the ideas in each chapter. Through an outsourcing site, I was connected with Croatian artist Damir Kundalic. His ability to take a very rough idea or sketch and transform it into something simple, fun, and memorable is remarkable. Thanks, Damir, you have a real gift there.

Finally, I want to thank everyone else who has helped me along my journey towards presence, including my partners, children, friends and colleagues. Every relationship - no matter how blissful or fraught - has taught me something about myself. Without you, I would not have become the person I am today. I love you all.

My Journey.

The Present is not a manual on how to be more successful or achieve more prosperity – there are enough of those out there already. *The Present* is written as a practical guide to help those searching for a way to experience more depth, meaning and connection in their lives. It is written to not only increase my own understanding and strengthen my own practice, but also as a vehicle to share insights and practices with those like me.

For many years, I was driven by the need to compete, to prove myself, to win – even when winning meant that I was left broken and empty. The urge to succeed seemed to eclipse all else, including my capacity to truly feel, to love or to simply be content with my life as it stood. This hunger for what I believed to be completeness, affected not only my state of mind, but also my physical health and my family.

I would watch on enviously as others delighted in the moment, laughing deeply or just smiling and giving thanks to another beautiful day unfolding. What was wrong with me? Why was it so hard for me to savour this, the simplest of life's true pleasures?

To cope with my disconnection, I attempted to fill the void with work, alcohol, TV and obsessive thinking. These poor substitutes afforded me the occasional reprieve from my island of separateness, but when the distractions faded and I came back down to earth, I was still here. In the end they only served to highlight the disconnection I felt between my inner state and the world outside of me.

Somehow, I had existed this way for decades. I was married and a proud father of three rambunctious young boys. But something was wrong, and I couldn't put my finger on it. I searched for solutions, both inside and outside of myself, reading dozens of spiritual and self-help books, attending seminars and even changing my work situation, but the feeling of lightness and connection continued to elude me. I grew increasingly disillusioned with my life and future. My work suffered. My relationship suffered. My health suffered. My family suffered.

It's said that 'at first the Universe taps you on the shoulder but, if you continue not to listen, it will smack you in the face!' This is what happened to me. Over a period of 5 years my life was turned upside down through family illness, financial challenges and, eventually, relationship breakdown. I was forced to *surrender control*, as the alternative was purgatory. I committed myself to focusing on the present moment so that I could keep myself calm. I picked up Barry Long's book *Stillness is the Way* and returned to old faithful's like Ram Dass' *Be Here Now*. I put time aside in both the morning and evening to still my mind.

Slowly but significantly, the beliefs that I had clung to for the past 30 years started to lose their power. The belief that I needed to be in a traditional family unit to be a good father. The belief that I needed to be in a relationship to feel like a whole person. The belief that I needed to accumulate a certain amount of wealth to be a worthwhile individual. I didn't realise quite how heavy all these beliefs had become until I no longer had to carry their weight.

The more I let go, the more my life began to change for the better: new work opportunities appeared, new relationships flourished, a new view of life formed. I started tackling difficulties in my life situation with improved perspective and understanding. Long-buried feelings bubbled up through me; I shed tears of joy and loss and found a deeper appreciation of life. I felt that warm feeling of compassion and love expanding through my chest, enlivening me. I became better able to share my secrets and vulnerabilities with those who cared for me.

As I formed a better relationship with the moment, I began my new journey, a journey with less self-analysis and more intuition, less self-doubt and more faith, less fear and more courage. It's an adventure with its own sets of highs and lows, but now at least I'm feeling the bumps in the road and the wind in my hair. Today, my only destination is towards a stronger connection to the moment I am in. I find that this tends to take care of the rest.

I hope you enjoy this book.

Who Is This Book For?

This book is written for the *everyday guru*, the regular guy or gal, the person who is busy going about life and doing his/her best not to hurt anyone in the process.

This book is for those who have no desire to sit meditating in lotus position for hours and who feel slightly uncomfortable – even slightly defensive – when spirituality is discussed.

This book is for those who are too busy living life to ponder its meaning (but would like to know the answer anyway).

This book is for people who make it through work by focusing on 'clock-off' time and who often turn to alcohol to help ease the burden of everyday life.

This book is for people who feel that, whilst they have tried very hard, real fulfilment and happiness still somehow eludes them.

This book is for people who have dealt with difficult circumstances in their lives and who have managed to survive – but not quite thrive.

This book is for those who look on longingly at others basking in the throes of joy and ask themselves, 'Why can't I do that?'

This book is for people who know it's time to put themselves first for a change, to be more kind to themselves and practice more self-love.

This book is for you and me – we are the *everyday gurus* who, by changing ourselves also change the lives of those around us for the better.

This book is for a better world by inspiring a better you.

How to Use this Book.

Please read this book as you will, but should you be interested in my intent, here 'tis:

The Present is split into four parts; you may choose to read them sequentially or to open it at *any* page at random and read whatever catches your attention and interest – you'll know if it speaks to you very quickly. If it doesn't, simply turn to another page until you find an idea or practice that does resonates with you.

The illustrations are intended to reinforce and underline the ideas presented; they will enable you to recall the most relevant and powerful lessons. Sit with them, dwell on both them and the message, carry them with you through your day and bring them to mind when a stronger connection to the present moment is desired.

At the end of each Present Principle, you'll find a 'Freedom Phrase'. This is a sound-bite statement that may be used to help you to activate the principle in your world, to escape the clutches of negative thinking and bring you back into the moment. Shortcuts to pertinent principles and practices are also listed, so feel free to skip from front to back, middle to front or whichever way your interest or intuition leads you. Let curiosity be your guide.

When you're struck with the urge to act (you might have an image flash into your mind or feel a stirring of energy in your tummy), then please do so. Don't allow yourself to overthink or overrule this spontaneous prompt to take action, as action always exists in the present (even though it can be driven by events in the past). When you combine inspired action with strong intent, you can move mountains.

Leave this handbook lying around to flick through when you have a few free minutes or if you're looking for a higher perspective on your life events. Draw out an idea or two whenever you need them and apply them as you see fit. Encourage others to also partake of the ideas and messages, and breathe further life into them through discussion.

But above all, please use this book as a means to help yourself to *let go* – to let go of all the mental strain and tension you have collected – to let go of your connection to the past and just let yourself *be* for a while. You deserve all the peace, joy and fulfilment that can only be experienced when you are completely present.

This is your moment.

PART 1:

BE PRESENT

Where Are You?

'Be here now.'
Baba Ram Dass, Guru, LSD Explorer

Have you ever found yourself driving or walking somewhere and, upon arriving at your destination, remembering little or nothing of the journey? How about your lunch today? Do you remember savouring the flavour, smell and texture of your food, or did you consume it on autopilot while your mind was off busying itself with other matters? Let's be honest, sometimes you can be standing directly in front of somebody who is talking to you, and you're *still* not there – instead your attention is focused on what you're going to say next or perhaps thinking about your own situation.

Whenareyouactually*here*?Howoftenisyourattentionfocused100%onthismoment?Ahandful of times a day? Once a day? Even less?

In a world ruled by the clock and teeming with technological distractions, the *quality of your attention* is your most precious asset, yet it is often squandered by compulsive thinking in a manner resembling an addict. Your mind has become conditioned to constantly surge with thought, lest you find yourself falling behind or slacking off in some way.

THE PRESENT.

Gandhi once said, 'There is more to life than simply increasing its speed'. The quality of your life should not be measured by the length of time you're here, but by the *depth of the moments that you are lucky enough to be here to experience*. How well you can accept and appreciate the moment you're in – no matter how it presents itself – will determine your sense of belonging and oneness with the world. This is what it means to 'be present', and it is the essence of being truly alive.

When you are completely present, one hundred percent of your energy and attention is at your disposal, allowing you to think more creatively, to be more spontaneous and to be better guided by your intuition. With this level of heightened connection, you are able to access your fullest potential, connecting with others, identifying new opportunities and experiencing breakthroughs in perspective.

The discipline of staying present involves consistently reminding yourself not to be distracted by thoughts about the future or the past. You've spent years feeding your mind and keeping the furnace fired with thought, so turning this off (or down) may seem impossible. If you aren't convinced, try taking a shower without planning your day or remembering what happened yesterday; just *be* in the shower – it's much harder than you think.

If you struggle with this, now is the time to make a commitment to *slow down*, not just physically but mentally, as well, and regain the power that comes when you exercise focused attention. When eating your meal, slow down to savour the aroma and texture and flavour. When in conversation with another, make a conscious decision to quieten your thoughts and give the person your undivided attention. See if you can remove that incessant and unnecessary pressure you task yourself with: to constantly be moving and thinking at light speed.

The more you practice redirecting your focus back into *this* moment, the more it becomes a habit, and the better you get at it. When you notice your mind wandering, try asking yourself, '*Where am I?*' and gently nudge your attention back into your immediate environment. This does not mean you are not still free to dream, reminisce or imagine, as all of this serves a purpose. It's the fear, worry and stress that you can do without. By checking in with yourself occasionally and asking, 'Where am I?', you are recognizing that you are disconnected from the moment and giving yourself the opportunity to become present again.

This is where the most powerful version of yourself always resides. Right here. Right now.

The Gift of the Present.

'Yesterday is history, tomorrow but a mystery.
But this moment is a gift
and that's why it's called the Present.'
Unknown

The Present is right now, this very moment. Everything that happens to you does so now. Your entire life is made up of billions of these precious moments, and it is here, in this never-ending stream of *now-ness*, that you'll find the key to escape the prison of self-doubt, and the gateway to true freedom.

Presence (or *being* present) is the mysterious quality that often appears to others as magnetic charisma, a warming charm that makes them feel safe. The people you love to spend time with – your friends, your family, your colleagues – are so loved because they allow you to sweep aside past troubles and future concerns, and just *be* yourself with them.

The most endearing quality that anyone can possess is to be completely and utterly present – to surrender to the moment so wholeheartedly that a deep peace from within emanates outwards from you, quieting and calming the world. In this state of grace, your inner connection resonates through to others, and you become a safe harbour for friends and loved ones to come and replenish themselves.

THE PRESENT.

When you are present, you are happy – it's impossible to be truly happy and *not* be present! The search for happiness is a trick of the mind, with the idea of happiness often being attached to external circumstances or objects, creating an illusionary sense of completeness. We say we're happy because we won this, achieved that, fell in love etc., but the satisfaction that comes from accomplishment is only ever fleeting and will quickly need to be replaced or topped up.

Real, soul-satisfying happiness comes from feeling as *one with life* – when we stop resisting and allow our natural state of joy to resonate through us. You've likely experienced these moments before; they are hard to forget as they sear into your memory. When you felt this depth of contentment, it was because you switched off your thinking mind and therefore had become vitally present.

In this heightened state of awareness, your intuition speaks to you clearly, enabling you to make decisions with certainty and conviction. Taking a leap of faith becomes easy when you do not fear the future; after all, the future is simply going to be another present moment for you to befriend.

When connected to the moment, you instinctively want to help others. You feel compassion and understanding for those you may have once judged harshly. You strive to create unity and connection over mistrust and separation that may otherwise exist. Like when a stone is thrown into pond, the ripple effect resonates out to others, giving them permission to be themselves, to be real.

Your presence is most certainly a gift to yourself, to others and to the world.

The Only Dance There Is.

'Nothing is more precious than being in the present moment. Fully alive. Fully aware.'
Thích Nhất Hạnh, Vietnamese Buddhist, Peace Activist, Speaker of Seven Languages.

You were born present, and your natural state of being is calm, generous and loving. In this state, you feel comfortable and secure, with the absence of fear and self-doubt allowing you to enjoy more laughter and a general lightness of being. You may experience this feeling when on vacation, or when you're in the company of good friends or loved ones, or perhaps when indulging in your favourite outdoor activity.

But life has a way of messing with your mojo; you get stuck in traffic, your partner criticises something you've done or your boss decides that those 8 hours of sleep you enjoy so much could be better spent at the office. If you're not mindful, it's easy to become defensive, surrender your calm and slip into a very negative headspace, leaving you upset, uptight and in pain.

Spiritual guru (and former Harvard professor) Ram Dass speaks of this in his book *The Only Dance There Is*. He says, 'Everything you do, whether you're cooking food or doing therapy or being a lover, you are only doing your own being, you're only manifesting how evolved a consciousness you are...that's the *only dance there is*.'

THE PRESENT.

Here, Ram Dass highlights the importance of focusing our attention and energy not so much on *what* we are doing (the objective or end goal), but on *how* we are doing it. The how is the interface between our physical and mental energy and the world around us. It's *how* we do *what we do* that reveals our current state of consciousness to the world.

The more we overlook the *how* in favour of the *what* (or outcome), the more disconnected we will become from the task, and the more resistance we will encounter. This is because the quality of any outcome is intricately tied to the level of focus and awareness we are applying to its creation. Every thought outside of the moment we are in – even if it's on the end goal that we desire so much – depletes the energy and resources available to us in order to realise its fullest potential.

It is *how* you do what you do – the level of awareness you bring to what you are doing – that determines the quality of your end result.

This is the 'dance' of the moment. It's about consciously choosing which step to take until you start to find your rhythm. The dance is never-endingly different and sometimes extremely challenging, but it is *your responsibility* to stay in step – no one else's.

Opportunities to practice occur all around us, for example, when stuck in traffic, you can choose to remain calm rather than succumb to anxiety or anger. Take a breath and allow yourself to relax, focus on what's in your control and let go of the rest – it may be hard, but what's the alternative? When you start to practice this in earnest, you'll start to realise that much of the drama you experience is caused by you simply resisting what *is* by wanting things to be different than they actually are.

Instead of seeing life's little (or big) challenges as painful obstacles holding you back, try viewing them as opportunities to learn more about managing your state of being, to learn a new dance. When you accept the situation you are in and do not succumb to self-sabotage and blame, you are successfully protecting your state and keeping yourself open and responsive. Once you get this, you'll experience a great sense of empowerment and ultimately, a great relief.

Little by little, you'll gain more control over the emotional rollercoaster that you have experienced thus far in life, and you'll likely start finding situations and people that once drove you mad have become quite menial, even laughable. You'll realise that, despite the natural ups and downs, you are able to let go a little more each time, and you'll start shimmying across the dance floor of life.

Your Gut Brain.

'If you listen to your body when it whispers, you will never have to listen to it scream.'
Unknown

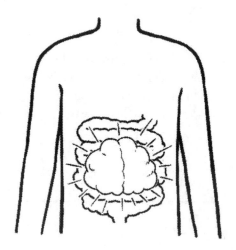

Science is always uncovering new and amazing facts about our biology. A fascinating finding over recent years has been the identification of a nerve that is thought to be primarily responsible for our mind/ body connection. While there was an *assumed* link between our mind and body, scientists can now map the physiology and explain how information is transmitted between these two energy centres.

Your central nervous system (which is responsible for 'autopilot' functions such as heart rate, respiration, digestion, etc.) acts as a *two-way* communication channel between your body and your brain. Its finely tuned sensors pick up on cues and send signals to your brain that impact stress, mood, decision-making and memory.

The digestive system has a particularly high concentration of these nerve endings (or sensors), and this is why it's often referred to as the 'gut' or 'second brain'. You often get feelings in your gut, or tummy, about people or situations. Some call it intuition, but it is actually the 'gut brain' at work. You've likely experienced a situation where you have overridden this intuition (or 'gut instinct') with intellect or reasoning, only to find out later that you should have listened to your gut.

Often the best response to a situation lies in what we *feel*, and not what we *think*.

THE PRESENT.

When a threat is encountered, your body jumps into action mode, activating the three Fs (fight/flight/freeze). Your heart rate and breathing increase, your pupils widen to absorb more visual information, and your digestion is put on hold as blood rushes to your muscles, arming them for a response. All of this happens automatically and instantaneously to prepare you to deal with the threat. It doesn't matter if the threat is real (a rabid dog running at you) or imagined (anxiety over bills or money); your body arms itself just the same.

If you live with chronic stress, either inside or outside of work, your body *never* has a chance to work properly. All the signals being sent out by your overworked mind place all systems in your body on high alert. Stress hormones are released to deal with the stress, inflaming the body and upsetting your natural resting and healing modes.

When the threat subsides and you feel safe once again, your brain triggers the release of a new set of calming hormones through your nervous system, which act to take your body out of high alert mode and promote a sense of calm, relaxation or sleep. You have the ability to control this calming reflex through a little-known nerve that facilitates a two-way superhighway of information, running between your mind and your body: **the vagus nerve.**

The Vagus Nerve.

'There is a voice that doesn't use words. Listen.'
Rumi

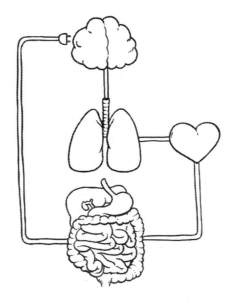

The vagus nerve is thought to be the primary nerve responsible for our mind–body connection, running down the back of our neck from our brain, through our throat, heart, lungs, liver and digestive organs. Vagus is Latin for 'wandering', as the nerve *wanders* throughout the different vital organs and areas of our body.

Scientific tests have proven that directly stimulating the vagus nerve slows the heart rate, lowers blood pressure and reduces stress hormones in the bloodstream. The vagus nerve acts like a 'reset button', sending out information to the rest of the body that everything's fine – we can now resume normal programming.

The vagus nerve can either be stimulated artificially via surgical means (which is done in some cases to treat epilepsy) or naturally through focus and practice. One technique that has been proven to directly activate the vagus nerve is *diaphragmatic breathing*, a deep breathing that is drawn in through the abdomen, where many of the nerve endings from the 'wandering' nerve end up.

By learning how to control the switch to this 'power cord' running between your cognitive insights and gut instincts, you will feel more in control of your outer world because you are mastering your inner world.

THE PRESENT.

You will feel more relaxed and centred, experiencing a deeper level of connection and empathy for others. This is the reason that the vagus nerve is also known as the 'compassion' nerve.

This book has been written to help you stimulate this nerve and access more peace and presence. The principles and practices contained within will allow you to better manage the interflow or information running up and down this most vital connection, helping you to take control of your thoughts and feelings and, ultimately, your world.

Let's get started…

PART II:

THE STATE WE'RE IN

The State We're In.

*'We cannot solve our problems
with the same level of thinking that created them.'*
Albert Einstein, Theoretical Physicist, Avid Gardener

We are alive in the wealthiest period that the world has ever known; hundreds of millions of people now live lives that were once only possible for kings and their royal subjects, enjoying plentiful food, large comfortable homes and the freedom to choose the career – and spouse – of their choice.

Yet, even with the bountiful riches and opportunity now at our disposal, we have been unable to eliminate the pain and suffering from our day-to-day experiences. You only need to read the newspaper, watch the news or chat with a neighbour to know this to be true. Despite our current prosperity, many people are still struggling. Struggling to find a balance. Struggling to be happy. Struggling to live.

While we no longer have to endure the physical stress of our forbearers, we do have to cope with more mental stress than at any other time in history, and it's coming at a cost. The World Health Organisation (WHO) has predicted that by 2030, depression will account for the highest level of disability accorded any physical or mental disorder in the world. Billions of dollars are being spent every year to treat this and other mood-related disorders, yet rates of depression and anxiety-related disorders keep soaring.

In Australia, suicide continues to be the largest single cause of injury-related death – everyday, at least six Australians die and at least *thirty* people attempt to take their own life. Despite all the focus this issue receives, and the great work being done by organisations such as Black Dog Institute and Lifeline over recent years, Australians are shockingly more likely to die by suicide than by skin cancer.

The use of addictive drugs (legal and illegal) has also reached epidemic proportions. More people are addicted to, and dying from, a wider range of drugs than ever before. Worldwide, the use of opiates, cocaine and cannabis has all increased. In Australia, illicit drug use increased over 13% between over the 3 years to 2010. In 2011, a report by the Global Commission on Drugs found that the 'global war on drugs has failed'.

More of us are also turning to alcohol. Australia's love affair with liquor started with the rum brought over by convict ships, but has bloomed into a national occupation, with alcohol a mandatory inclusion at every celebration, and often being consumed daily. A study by the Productivity Commission in 2010 stated that the cost of the harmful effects of alcohol on society was almost $15 billion – more than *twice* the revenue generated from alcohol taxation.

Wearedrinkinganddruggingourwaytooblivion.Wearedepressedandstressedtounprecedented levels. We are committing suicide. Something is *very* wrong with how we are living.

We are facing the biggest mental health crisis in our history, yet despite our best efforts, it's getting worse. We must find a way to escape our current paradigm – to let go and alleviate the pressure that we subject ourselves to and regain the peace and stillness within. If we can do this, we will not only drastically improve our own lives, but also the lives of those around us, as our inner connection resonates out into the world through our actions, reactions and behaviour.

It is now both urgent and imperative that we become more mindful about the way we exist and act, to take regular pit-stops along the information superhighway we are zooming down and admire the scenery – even for a moment or two. In the end, it's all we ever have.

The Mind at Large.

'Men are not prisoners of fate, but only prisoners of their own minds.'
Franklin D. Roosevelt, 32nd President of the United States, Stamp Collector

As soon as your alarm sounds, your brain clicks and whirrs back into gear, and before you even stumble out of bed, you've mentally calculated the exact number of times you can press snooze before you'll be running late for work! Within minutes – or even seconds – of opening your eyes, you're reaching for your trusty smartphone, checking emails, messages, social media updates and news cycles. And all of this happens before you've even brushed your teeth.

You rush through the morning ritual of getting yourself, and perhaps your family, ready for the day ahead, while feeling the pressure of the clock urging you to speed things up, to move ever more quickly. Once out the door, there is little time to relax; instead, your thoughts surge forward into the day ahead – to the appointments you have, the deadlines you must meet or the outstanding issues needing to be resolved.

Throughout the day, your thought-speed only continues to gain momentum, fuelled by the frantic pace of technology and competition. Your mind is now firmly in the driver's seat, and the rest of you (your physical and emotional centres) are relegated to the passenger seat. They hang on for dear life as your mind takes your body on a high-speed joyride, and you keep on adding fuel to the fire; increasing your tempo with hits of coffee, energy drinks and chocolate fixes to keep the necessary sugar flowing to your brain, as it nears terminal velocity.

THE PRESENT.

You are now a Mind at Large; a rampaging cluster of unrestrained thought, fully detached from the present moment, and rollicking, unchecked and unrestrained throughout the day.

Finally, knock-off time comes, yet even the time spent on the way home can't be called downtime because you're still stuck in your head, regurgitating endless strains of thoughts created throughout the day – papers read…calls made…emails sent…and now you're making plans for the next day.

When you arrive back home, you quickly reach for the wine, the chocolate, the remote – anything that might help distract you or slow the momentum and bring you back down to earth. When you eventually fall into bed, exhausted from all the mental activity, you are frustrated to find your mind still whirring, not ready to stop yet. It may take hours, or even sleeping pills, to finally shutdown your thoughts so you can get some sleep.

But even now your mind keeps on turning, with your dreams piecing together random threads of thoughts, feelings and emotions experienced throughout the day into a jumble of disjointed action sequences, resembling some B-grade art-house movie. When you *finally* reach a state of dreamless sleep, it's now only a handful of hours until the cycle starts again, and your mind is back at large.

When was the last time you gave your mind a chance to rest, to stop thinking, even for a few minutes? What steps are you willing to take to redress the balance?

Mind-Time.

It's easy to get lost in your thoughts. It starts with one innocent thought, which leads to another...and then another...and yet another, until you're so far away from the seed-thought that you've forgotten where it was that you began! When you're in your thoughts, you're separate from the present moment; you're away in an imagined world created only in your mind. How you feel about what you're thinking could be either good or bad, but it is not *real* because it's not *now*.

That's not to say that there's anything *wrong* with thinking; it's just that that your thought-energy is being invested outside of the moment (and into your imaginings about the past and/or the future), diminishing the energy available to you. As your best life experiences happen when you are present, if you're lost in thought or worry, it's easy to miss the potential and depth inherent in each moment or situation as it presents itself.

There is a name for this type of unnecessary internal rambling - Mind-time.

Mind-time is time spent thinking about (or dwelling upon) the past and/or the future. You may be reflecting on times gone by or anticipating what's yet to come; either way your attention and energy are invested outside of *this* moment, and while this may often be pleasurable, it removes you from your centre of power which always exists in the present.

THE PRESENT.

Mind-time exists outside of what Eckhart Tolle in his seminal book *The Power of Now* calls 'clock time'. He describes clock-time as having a functional purpose and being necessary to help us regulate our bodies, map our days, and set and achieve goals. Mind-time, however, serves no functional purpose other than to rob us of valuable energy that would be better applied to the moment at hand.

Whether you are recalling happier times (which typically were only so *because* you were present) or experiencing sadness brought about by reflecting on old hurts or disappointments, either way you are focusing your energy and attention back in time to a moment which has long since passed. When you dream (or worry) about the future, it's all imagination – a story about what *might* happen. You may feel excitement or anticipation or stress or dread, all physical feelings felt in the present but based solely on your imaginings.

Most certainly, it's the negative and unhelpful thoughts about the past and future which make you feel bad and diminish your quality of life, as they not only steal energy and vitality from the moment you are in, but also cause you stress and pain. It may be tempting to believe that happy thoughts are safe and should be encouraged, although these too can take you away from where you are, pitting the current moment against *perceived* happier times and often creating a wishful state of being 'back there' rather than 'right here'.

It is your ability to be at peace with *this* moment, however it may appear, that will enable you to avoid getting lost in mind-time and help you experience the lightness of being that comes from being more present. Even if you find the moment extremely challenging, by accepting it as it is and not getting stuck on how it *should be*, you're able to deal with it with more conviction and clarity because you haven't cluttered your mind with unnecessary, erroneous or negative thoughts.

This concept may seem overwhelming at first, as it's likely that much of your adult life has evolved around the notion that your mind contains all the answers. All you need to do for now is to make a distinction between mind-time and clock-time and become more aware of those times when you get lost in your thoughts. When you start to notice yourself doing this, you are already halfway there, as your conscious awareness is now bearing witness to the fickle nature of your mind.

The practices later in this book will help you to reduce the time spent in Mind-time.

Prisoner of Time.

'It is not length of life, but depth of life what matters in the end.'
Ralph Waldo Emerson, Poet, Writer, Transcendentalist

For many in our busy world, time is their master – and what a tough taskmaster it can be. With time as your master, you feel guilty taking a break or a holiday when there's still work to be done. With time as your master, you tend to focus on achieving too many things at once, and thereby dilute the quality of your output. With time as your master, your life is not your own; it is owned by the *possibility* of a better future – one which exists outside of the present moment.

When you're a prisoner of time, the present moment is merely viewed as a stepping-stone toward a future you, one whom you imagine will be better, richer, prettier and happier. In this way of viewing the world, the present moment only serves as something to be tolerated in order to obtain your desired objectives, and the value of this moment is whittled down to merely a *means to an end*.

You become so fixated by the notion of happiness existing somewhere off in the future that your inner state is constantly left on edge and under strain, seldom allowed to restore itself to its natural state of stillness. The prison of time keeps you in a constant state of anticipation and therefore rules out the possibility of being at peace with the way things are. You're left tired, anxious, disconnected from yourself and – perhaps most frustratingly of all – least able to enjoy your much-anticipated goals when they are finally brought to fruition.

The first step toward escaping from the prison of time is to understand that the shackles that bind you are entirely self-imposed.

No one has sentenced you and locked you up. You have *chosen* to commit yourself to the quality of life you have by attaching feelings of fulfilment and completeness onto some distant goal. But don't beat yourself up; many people in our society live this way – it has almost become the status quo and can be extremely hard to resist.

Just as you (unwittingly) allowed time to become your overlord, you are also free to choose a different path, a path where time is not your enemy, but an important ally. You can choose a path that gives you the ability to dream and plan, to set and achieve goals, but at the same time maintains your attention in the present. Yes, it's important to keep an eye on the prize, but it is even more important to immerse yourself fully in every moment that comes your way, as this is where the seeds of opportunity are planted that will help you to expedite your plans.

If you judge your worth based solely on the possibility of future success, you will always end up with a hollow victory. Even when you have accomplished your goal, you'll still have time egging you on, prodding you to get more, do more, have more, to be more, making you feel that *this* moment still is not enough – that *you* are not enough.

By befriending the moment (which is timeless), you start exploring the depth of time, layer after layer of potential and possibility. You connect to a new perspective, a new paradigm and a world outside the constrictive walls of time. This is true freedom.

Pain & Gain.

'You can't just love the gain, the good times,
because by loving the good, you bring the opposite.'
Barry Long, Spiritual Teacher, Writer, Former Australian Press Secretary

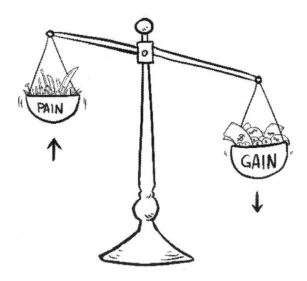

You celebrate when you finally land that dream job. You skip down the street after meeting that wonderful new partner. You feel proud when you achieve a highly prized social status. The high that comes from acquiring a long-desired goal can be quite intoxicating, and it's easy to feel justifiably rewarded or special, like the gods are finally smiling on you and that you just can't put a foot wrong.

But what happens when the very same things fall from your grasp?

You are made redundant. Your partner leaves you. Your reputation is in tatters (thanks to a careless late-night Facebook post…). This sense of loss can be enough to make you question not only your own worth, but also life's worth. How could this happen to you? How could life be so cruel and nasty? What did you do to deserve *all* this?

Barry Long speaks of this in his wonderful book *Stillness is the Way*. He makes the observation: 'This is how many people experience their lives: up one minute and down the next, like a seesaw. They oscillate between varying degrees of pain and gain, and if they're lucky, they might experience a narrow band between these two extremes in which they're not wanting or mourning – they are simply happy just to *be*.'

This pain and gain syndrome is created by your mind as a way to bolster your ego and to help you compete in what the mind sees as a *hostile* world. Like a race, in order to avoid suffering the lows of loss (which to the mind makes you weak and less likely to survive), you must struggle for and pursue winning at all costs. If you do manage to cross the finish line first, then you may relish the short-term elation of the crowd. If you lose, you may be down on yourself, with that little voice in your head saying: *I should've won, I'm not good enough* or *I should have practiced harder.*

Buddhist teachings speak of 'non-attachment', the ability to accept something without identifying with it or attaching yourself to it. The more you attach yourself to something, the more it hurts when it is lost, taken away or simply moves on. This is *not* to say that you shouldn't enjoy (or indeed love) what you have in your life – simply don't allow it to define you.

You are intrinsically valuable just as you are. You don't need anything external to validate your worth. This is an illusion and the cause of much pain and misery.

To escape this cycle of pain and gain, become aware of all the attachments in your life: your house, your car, your spouse, your job, your looks – even your opinions, beliefs or the need to always be heard or be right. Look at these attachments through the filter of how much they define who you think you are. Do you think you're successful or better than others because you have a professional job? Do you believe you are doomed to failure because you don't have a college degree? Do you believe that you are more worthy than others because you drive a nice car? Are you less worthy if you drive a clunker?

These questions require your ego (or 'social identity') to take a back seat and force you to view yourself stripped of the things you use to define who you *think* you are. The more you rely on external factors to define *you*, the more attached you become to them, which results in more pain when they eventually get old, get stolen, die, break or are destroyed.

Effort & Struggle.

*'Although we may wish for more or strive to do better than we have,
in these times it is enough to keep your soul.'*
Eric Micha'el Leventhal, Author, Keen Adventurer

We are told that 'happiness is a journey and not a destination', but this seems at odds with what's being sold to us on a daily basis. We are bombarded with marketing messages that try to sell us on the idea that, with *this* new acquisition, we'll have made it. We tell ourselves, 'When I get there, (or this, or them), *then* I'll be happy!' Rather than being content with things as they stand, we experience an underlying and ongoing sense of unease with what we have or where we are, leaving us to continually be thinking about what we could or *should* be doing or acquiring.

You may tell yourself that you're struggling this hard so you can provide for your family or perhaps to improve your financial situation. You may believe that if you struggle hard enough, you'll eventually have the all the things needed in life to finally be content. But all too often, it's all just a mirage. Being content is available to you right now – it's a state of mind you can choose, a state of being that already exists within you.

Sometimes you struggle simply because *you believe* that's what is expected of you.

THE PRESENT.

Happiness simply doesn't emerge through struggle; have you ever tried to be happy? You can't force it. Happiness typically arises in the *absence* of effort and struggle, when you're content just *being* and when you accept the situation as it stands. Think of the most genuinely happy person you know; what do they value? Are they constantly talking about the new house they're buying or the business they've just created, or are they less concerned with these things and more enriched by service to others, kindness and compassion? Even if they *are* facing hardships, do you see them struggling, or do they seem to handle the situation with grace and acceptance?

We would do well to find this level of acceptance within ourselves and resist the compulsion to always be striving for something better. Once we come to realise that much of our struggle is actually an internal battle to find peace and fulfillment, and that we can access this without all the strife, then we are able to alleviate some of the underlying dissatisfaction within ourselves, our relationships and our world in general.

What would it be like to believe that you are perfect just as you are, and to know that any attempt to become *more* perfect is a waste of energy? What if you stopped struggling and discovered that the peace you seek already exists within you, and what if the things you pine for so desperately started moving toward you rather than being pushed further away? Deep down you know it is possible – you may have even experienced it before; that job opportunity appeared just when you had given up, or that new relationship that started just around the time you decided you were content just being in your own company for a while.

Of course, none of this means giving up on your own personal evolution, or to stop challenging yourself to grow and develop. You still need to meet the external stresses with courage and resilience if you're to become all you can be. It's more about letting go of the neediness, the constant wanting and fixation on the future, and instead, making your connection with this moment a priority.

Stop the struggle and just be.

The Having World.

'It is preoccupation with possessions, more than anything else,
that prevents us from living freely and nobly.'
Bertrand Russell, Philosopher, Mathematician, Activist

We live in a 'having' world, one in which we're judged by many according to what possessions, status or money we have. If we have a million dollars, we are said to be *worth* something. If we have a billion dollars, we are revered like a god! If we have a position that enables us to wield power and influence over others, we're often seen as more worthy than someone who hasn't obtained a similar status.

But what if we have little or nothing? What if we have few material possessions, hold no status or have very little sway over others? Are we still worthwhile human beings? It's easy for us to feel inadequate living in a society that constantly sells the message that we must *have* more to *be* more. But just where did this perspective come from? And how did it become so pervasive?

The belief that self-worth is synonymous with net worth is a relatively recent condition in our evolution on this earth, only surfacing after the Industrial Revolution, and is found predominantly in societies where the economics are based on the ownership of private property. That is to say, the more we make life about ownership, they more we are able to possess and wield power over others.

The word 'private' is derived from the Latin *privare*, meaning 'to deprive of'. In other words, the owner of an item, or the one who possesses an item, has the authority to deprive others of it. In this way, the more I own, the more I may deny others the rights to use, thereby giving me power and status. It therefore seems natural that, in a society that values acquisition and ownership over community and contribution, those who haven't amassed enough possessions (and even some who have) will often be left feeling unfulfilled.

When meeting a high net-worth individual, it's not uncommon to feel nervous or anxious, as you look to balance your worth against theirs. If this analysis makes you feel inferior, it's not because you are any less of a human being (you are of equal intrinsic value), it's just that your conditioned beliefs about worth cause you to feel somehow *less than* rather than *equal to*. This belief not only restricts the potential of the interaction, but also can make you appear inauthentic as you struggle to portray a person you think they'd rather see.

In a having world, everything must be possessed; everything must become our property so that we may be 'enough'.

You associate so much of who you think you are with both your tangible and intangible possessions. You collect books, pictures, spoons, even memories and relationships, and use all of these to form your sense of self. But the more you collect, the more you seem to want, and this can easily turn from being a healthy pursuit into a dysfunction.

In his seminal book *To Have or to Be*, Eric Fromm underscores the issue of language by illustrating that prior to the Industrial Revolution people would say, 'I *am* troubled', but today we say, 'I *have* a problem.' We also say, 'I *have* an idea' instead of 'I just thought of something', or 'I *have* a headache' instead of 'My head hurts'. In our 'having' world, even intangible concepts like problems and ideas become possessions that we somehow now own!

Descartes' famous dictum stated, 'I *think*, therefore I am', yet in our society, it might be rephrased as, 'I *have*, therefore I am.' In a having world, your primary (and often unconscious) desire is to pursue more, get more and ultimately own more, even if it costs you your inner peace, loving relationships and sanity.

Having vs. Being.

'Our goal should be to BE much, not to HAVE much.'
Karl Marx, Economist, Communist, Social Butterfly

There is no doubt that in order to survive, we must *have* things such as shelter, food, transportation, etc. The act of 'having' is not in itself bad or wrong, it only becomes destructive when it becomes the main focus of our life: I must *have* in order to be *happy*.

But you cannot *have* happiness; you can only *be* happy.

Authentic happiness is a state that arises from within us when we feel safe and present, and is independent of what we own and of our position in society. It's no coincidence that many of the most naturally joyous people on this planet are found in developing countries, where the smiles on the children's faces and the genuine warmth of the adults stand in stark contrast to their very basic living conditions. Why are they so happy? Because they are content just to *be present* and haven't (perhaps yet) succumbed to the incessant drive for more and better. Even when receiving little, they are extremely grateful.

Being is your natural state and is always available to you. When you are being yourself, you are not concerned with *what* you have or *who* you are, instead you're simply happy expressing your true nature. In these moments, you're more creative, spontaneous, courageous, humorous and action-orientated. The people you most love and admire in this world are so loved because of their connection and comfort with their own state of being.

When you're in the having mode, your interactions with others can be calculated and self-focused; conversations are seen as a means to an end, and you only engage in interactions to progress your own agenda. You only focus on what the other person is saying to the degree that you need to keep track of the conversation, and so you can identify where your relevant point fits in.

In the being mode, you are more open and spontaneous with your interactions. This state allows you to read the full spectrum of communication capturing more of the nuances, tonality and intent. Even those stuck in the 'having mode' will eventually start yielding to your presence as you connect with them from a place of authenticity and centredness. The wonderful thing about being is that there is no need to *try* – unless you're trying to be someone you're not, which comes across as inauthentic and will be evident to those around you.

The having mindset is predominantly concerned with the *past* and the *future*. People stuck in the having mode constantly talk about their achievements, their relationships, their money or their social status. They find their identity in what *was* or what *will be* – not what *is*. When the desire to have is directed at the future, it becomes a dominating force, overshadowing the experience of the moment and creating a climate of constant stress and striving. Attaining the goal or possessing the object becomes so compelling that the present moment is whittled down to a stepping-stone with no intrinsic value.

In the being mode your attention and senses are in flow with the moment, where the opportunities exist to create your desired future. You remain agile and ready to take spontaneous action owing to not being constrained by unnecessary or irrelevant thoughts. You are able to recognise and enjoy simple moments that may well become fond memories. You'll bridge gaps between yourself and others that will enrich your life and the lives of those around you.

When you are content just *being* you, you'll find that others look at you with fresh eyes; they may even ask: 'What have you changed about yourself...is it your hair?' As your energy shifts, your ability and willingness to form strong connections with others increases. You feel more confident of yourself and more satisfied with where you are in life. Rather than trudging along on the *having* treadmill, you regain a childlike curiosity, playing more and worrying less. You see opportunities every day to deepen your experience.

Choosing to live in the *being* mode awakens feelings of true aliveness and connectivity, which is the very essence of being *present*.

It's time now to start the journey home…

PART III:

PRESENT PRINCIPLES

Shield Your State.

'Keep calm and carry on.'
British Government Propaganda Slogan, WW2

In a hectic world, it can be hard to keep yourself centred. Problems can appear out of nowhere. Dramas unfold. Situations just end up stressing you out. It's easy to succumb to the noise all around you, to connect with it emotionally and take it on as your own. But by doing this, you are unwittingly allowing your *external conditions* to infiltrate your *inner state*, ultimately costing you energy, focus and motivation.

Your natural state is one of stillness and calm. It's your default setting and exists as a constant in you unless you permit something (your thoughts or external stimuli) to disturb it. If you've ever left your phone in a taxi or emailed the wrong file to an important customer, you'll know how fast your sense of calm can turn into stress, anguish and bodily pain – almost instantly.

When you allow your state to be influenced by outside forces, you will find that your adrenaline surges, your heart rate increases and your ability to think rationally is momentarily suspended. You end up surrendering your best defence, which is to stay centred and maintain a calm disposition in order to solve for the situation. It's tempting to blame the outside circumstances for making you feel this way, but the truth is that you are *always* in control of your state, in fact, it's the *only* thing that you can truly control.

Don't fool yourself into thinking that how you *feel* is at the mercy of outside forces.

When you allow outside conditions to dictate your internal state, you become like a small ship adrift in a wild ocean, being tossed and turned by every passing swell. This is a codependent relationship where you allow the situations or people around you to influence how you feel, and ultimately to dictate the quality of your life.

When the external controls the internal, both your emotions and your physical body suffer. A disrupted internal state manifests itself as tension headaches, a weakened immune system, depression or anxiety. You then carry this trapped condition into other environments, like your home, your work or in your relationships – and often releasing it unwittingly at the most inopportune times.

So what's the remedy?

You must remind yourself that you always have power over your state. If a situation is making you feel bad, understand it's because *you* are allowing it. You always have two options, either attempt to change the situation or accept it as is to avoid creating further resistance, tension and pain. Reacting to an angry person with anger is a sure sign that you have let *their condition* dictate *your state*, which does little to solve the issue at hand. Cursing at the traffic when you're running late for an appointment is also a breach of state and will prevent you from being your best for the rest of the day.

Whatever the situation, remind yourself that it will eventually pass, and in letting it pass without attaching yourself to it, you will see the situation as it is, a small ripple that you can easily navigate through as captain of your ship and master of your state.

Freedom Phrase: 'This too shall pass.'

Also see: Let Go – page 43

And try this practice: Just Breathe – page 81

Stop Overthinking.

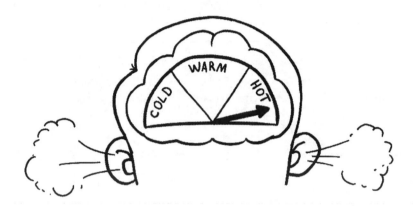

You *love* to think, it's a rush – almost like a drug. You love trying to work everything out, to find the secret formula to your success, wealth, health and happiness. You've been led to believe that a logical solution exists out there, so you keep your brain busy darting from one idea or fad to the next, looking for the missing pieces of the puzzle, for the pieces that will complete the picture, for the picture that will complete you.

The compulsion to constantly have to work things out is born of fear, a fear of the unknown, of failure, of rejection. You might believe you can reduce your anxiety by controlling your future, but you can't control your future just by just *thinking* about it. Your future is shaped by the actions you take in the here and now, by how you respond to *this* moment.

Stop trying to work things out all the time – give your mind and body a break.

Do you really need to ruminate over your problems while walking down the street, playing with the kids or resting in bed? How does this help you? Your intuitive mind operates best when it's relaxed and open – not pushed to the point of burnout. By overthinking and overcomplicating issues, you sap your creativity and deplete your body's natural vitality.

It's okay to tell yourself, 'There's nothing to work out right now' and to give yourself permission to be still. When a problem does arise, trust that you'll have the wherewithal to take the best action you can at the time, and save yourself the strain of needlessly overthinking it beforehand.

THE PRESENT.

There's no point in lying awake at night thinking, 'What will I do if…?' If there is no problem right now, there's no need to dwell upon it. If there is no action to take, then *you must let it go*. Attack only the challenges in the moment, as this is the best time to find the solution. Don't try to solve all the problems of the future like some sort of time-travelling warrior, as doing so will only disrupt your state and limit your ability to respond in full power.

Once you give up trying to work everything out, you'll find that everything is still okay. The sun still rises. The world does not end. Things start to slow down a bit and you begin to regain some perspective. This does not mean that you won't still encounter challenges in your path (you most certainly will), but you won't need to work them out. All you need to do is ask yourself, 'What can I do?' and then respond simply and appropriately in the moment.

Stop the feverish activity of the mind that tries to solve imaginary problems. That tension in your shoulders, in your scalp, everywhere in your body is caused by your mind trying to project you out of this moment, away from being yourself. Stay in the moment. Remain alert and self-aware, for it is out of *this* moment that your future will be forged.

Freedom Phrase: 'What needs to be happening *is* happening; therefore, I am at peace.'

Also see: Take Action – page 50

And try this practice: Counting Breaths – page 115

Lead with Intention.

'Attention symbolises the aiming of the archer...intention is the target.'
Buddhist Expression

From time to time, we all lose sight of what's most important to us. Perhaps, work (or school) pressures have taken over your life, or the chaos of a young family has left you exhausted and scrambling. In situations like these, you can start to question your life, to question your sanity, and feelings of anxiety and hopelessness can set in.

To regain your perspective, it's helpful to create a balance between planning for the future and continuing to stay connected to the present. The former requires *intention* and the latter requires *attention*, two dynamic concepts that must coexist harmoniously to provide us with focus, motivation and inspiration.

Intention speaks to your purpose, and it often presents itself as an envisaged or desired future outcome. Your intention provides a marker for where you want to be, and once this destination is programmed in, it acts much like a GPS, helping to guide the progress towards your goal. *Attention*, on the other hand, is your awareness of, and connection to, the here and now. It's the spotlight you shine onto whatever, or whomever, is in front of you.

To best understand the interplay of attention and intention, it is helpful to imagine an archer preparing to launch an arrow. *Attention* symbolises the aim of the archer, the focusing part of awareness: the feel of the bow in the hand, the tension in the string, one's bodily state, etc. *Intention* is the target; it's where the archer intends to land the arrow. It is clearly pictured as a future outcome (e.g. hitting the bullseye), but only focused attention in the aiming will make it possible to connect. *Action* is the archer's arrow, the physical motion that leads to the intention being realized.

Withacleartarget,laser-likeattentionandaspecificactiontaken,thearcherhascreatedaprocess for reaching the desired goal.

If you find yourself constantly striving for things such as increased status or financial freedom, you can become so narrowly focused on your future success that your *attention* is disconnected from the moment and diverted towards some distant goal in the horizon. The act of doing this then diminishes your ability to experience the joy and contentment to be found in the present. The habit is formed where you survive today with the hope of a brighter, happier future tomorrow. Beware: it's a trap.

Conversely, you may find yourself lacking motivation and energy. Uncertainty over your future may leave you feeling depressed or 'stuck'. Here, *intention* is your saviour. As a wise man once stated: 'The secret to success is simple; there are only two steps; Step 1 – Get clear about what you want. Step 2 – Be willing to pay the price to get it. But unfortunately, *most people don't make it to Step 1!*' The message here is simple: start by getting clear about what you want by setting your intention and direction. Once you do this, your actions then have a pathway to follow.

While it's important to be clear on what you want to create in your life – be it more love, better health, prosperity or a new car – it is important to keep this grounded by maintaining your attention in the moment, while your subconscious does the heavy lifting.

By doing this, you'll find that your dreams and ambitions will turn into opportunities and achievements – sometimes as if by magic.

Freedom Phrase: *'Intention* in the future, *attention* in the present.'

Also see: See the Everyday Gurus – page 72

And try this practice: Notice the Moment – page 83

Simplify.

'Our life is frittered away by detail. Simplify, simplify.'
Henry David Thoreau, Author, Poet, Tax Resister

Think back to the happiest times in your life; what were you doing? Chances are that you were enjoying the basics of a simple life, perhaps relaxing with friends, holidaying with your family or running on a beach. If you were at work, you may have been engaged in achieving a worthy and well-defined milestone. Whatever the activity, you were likely unencumbered by complexity and worry, and completely absorbed in the moment.

But market economics calls us to strive for more and better, fuelling an underlying discontent with what we have and where we are at in our lives. It's easy to succumb to the notion that if we accumulate more we will be happier, but paradoxically having more often only creates more complexity, leading us to worry more.

One of the keys to staying present, happy and in tune with life is to constantly seek simplicity.

Simplicity is an attribute of the awakened mind, a mind that is unattached to the past or future, a mind that is open and receptive, much like a child's. An awakened mind sees issues from a clear perspective, free from self-doubt, judgment and especially conditioned patterns. Einstein addressed this idea when he said, 'If you can't explain it to a 6-year-old, then you don't really understand it yourself!'

THE PRESENT.

The best way to tackle any problem in life is to do so simply. You have no doubt encountered people who, by adopting a simple, pragmatic approach to an issue or challenge, have quickly been able to solve it simply and with minimal fuss, as well as achieving a far better outcome than you might have imagined possible. These people are able to rise above the noise and gain insight into solutions by accessing an intuition that can only be found when present.

Minimize the complexity wherever possible and avoid sweating the small stuff. While details matter, it is always the big picture that's most important to keep in mind, and so long as you are clear on what that looks like – and how to stay aligned with it – then the minor details are just that; small stuff. It's better to move forward without having resolved all the finer details than it is to get stuck. Progress is more important than perfection.

Oliver Wendell Holmes, a famed American poet, once said that 'For the simplicity on this side of complexity, I wouldn't give you a fig. But for the simplicity on the other side of complexity, for that I would give you anything I have.' He refers to the idea that while some complexity is necessary, even unavoidable, it's the search for the simplicity on the other side that leads to a sense of control and calm.

Look to simplify everything. Simplify your work by breaking it down into basic chunks, and focus on the most important piece first. Simplify your relationships by forgiving and moving past petty hurts and wrongs. Simplify your thinking by taking time out to quiet your mind and letting go of unhelpful and erroneous thoughts.

Above all, keep telling yourself that *life is simple* and always look out for the simple hidden on the other side of complexity. If you are unable to find it, that's ok; you can always choose to simply move away from it.

Freedom Phrase: 'Go slowly; be easy.'

Also see: Stop Overthinking – page 35

And try this practice: Rush of Appreciation – page 85

Challenge the Story.

'Thoughts are things — choose the good ones!'
Mick Doley, Creator of 'The Universe'

Whether you realize it or not, your worldview is primarily composed of stories you have heard and accepted over the course of your life. We all have a veritable library of stories that we tell ourselves in order to make sense of our world. Some stories are positive and life affirming, while others serve to distance us from others, or worse, perpetuate pain and suffering in our lives.

The tapestry of stories that we are surrounded by should not be underestimated. Aside from the stories that infiltrated our minds during our formative years (stories we made up to cope with a situation or that we were told by authority figures), we are also bombarded with new ones daily. The TV news shares stories on the state of the world. Our neighbours share stories about those *other* pesky neighbours. Our parents share stories about their failing health. We choose to accept or reject these stories, depending on the strengths of our own beliefs, the authority of the storyteller, or our current state of vulnerability.

Once you have accepted a story, it quickly becomes one of your beliefs and you will then seek out stories that align with this new belief as confirmation of it. Stories (and people that tell them) that do not align with these ideas are judged harshly and often summarily dismissed. This is the cause of much of our disharmony;

a divorcing of ourselves from our fellow beings and a separation from our own humanity via unexamined stories that we have come to accept as truth

Your 'truth' is made up of the meaning you have given to your life events. There are in fact two parts, firstly there is *what happens* to you, and secondly, there is the *story you tell yourself* about what happened to you - the event and the story are always *two separate things*. The event itself comes with no meaning attached – it is neither good nor bad – it just *is*. When you attach a story to what happened, you provide your own meaning, and it is this attachment that dictates how you feel about it afterwards.

We are all 'meaning-making machines', always looking to attach meaning to life events. To stay present and positive we must be conscious of the meaning we are making.

Having your partner leave you for someone else can be a devastating experience – or not – depending on the meaning you ascribe to it. It may be tempting to look for everything wrong in the other, to blame them, to feel a victim. This way of thinking fires up the ego, disrupts your state, and creates an internal storm of emotion that can leave you reeling for months – or even years. It can get so bad that it can lead you to a breakdown. It's much harder at the time to look at the new opportunity that that now exists to refresh your life, to meet new people, to take up new hobbies. Which story or mindset would make you feel better?

The above choices are neither 'wrong' or 'right', but the latter does tend to *work better*, helping you to bounce back, become stronger and feel happier in the long term. Power comes from understanding that you have a *choice*. You can choose the story that you tell yourself about *every situation* that arises in your life. The story you choose will eventually become your truth; so if you are unhappy with an event or life situation, try challenging the story you are telling yourself, and then be prepared to replace it with one that empowers rather than disempowers you.

Make challenging your story a regular habit and your world will transform.

Freedom Phrase: 'There is what happens, and *the meaning* I attach to what happens.'

Also see: Lose the Ego – page 67

And try this practice: Empowering Affirmations – page 99

Let Go.

'If you let go a little, you will have a little peace;
if you let go a lot, you will have a lot of peace;
if you let go completely, you will have complete peace.'
Ajahn Chah, Buddhist Monk, Diabetic

It may be hard to admit, but much of the emotional – and even physical – pain you have experienced in your life has come from your unwillingness to *let go* of things, be they be intangible things such as ideas or opinions, or tangible things such as material possessions, money or lovers. You struggle to let go because you feel you have *earned* what you are holding onto – and you often won't let them go without a struggle.

If the message of this book had to be summarized in a simple phrase, it would simply be 'let go'. While it is a simple concept, it can be so difficult in practice that many will never attempt it, preferring instead to grip onto tightly to the ideas and things that are weighing them down and pulling them slowly under.

While letting go requires no physical effort, it does require overriding deeply ingrained habits and beliefs, which can appear as an insurmountable, if not impossible, task. Some will literally cling onto their stories and beliefs right up until the bitter end, taking their emotional pain and justifications with them to the grave.

The good news is that, once you start examining this notion of 'letting go', you may find that you are already practicing it to a degree. You likely let go of (or forgive) the occasional poorly timed comment from a good friend or loved one. You may also have no issue letting go of your beloved furniture or car when you move overseas. You even may have already let go of those you once used to call 'friends' when they started to diminish the quality of your life, rather than enhance it.

But some things are much harder to let go of; letting go of your need for approval, letting go of the story that justifies you seeing yourself as 'right' (even when you are hurting others by doing this), letting go of your guilt. You can become so deeply associated with the things or thoughts that you are holding onto that they you see start to see them as your *truth*, rather than a thought or idea you are holding onto about yourself or your situation. It then becomes very hard to let go of this *truth*, as it involves letting go of part of your identity, or ego.

Family gatherings are often a catalyst for tension and arguments as parents – who have held onto and become identified with their role as organisers and caregivers – still try to parent and advise their now adult children, even after the requirement for doing so has long since passed. Conversely, the same may be said for the adult male who still feels the need to be mothered and doted on by his busy spouse. Both situations can create a great deal of disharmony, with the root cause lying in the refusal to let go of a past role or notion.

Not letting go of things inhibits your natural energy flow and creates feelings of heaviness and separation. The emotional strain caused by holding on is experienced as a general malaise, mild depression or even chronic fatigue. The underlying mental strain may become so acute that it transmutes into physical symptoms such as digestive and musculoskeletal disorders. Western medicine is only now beginning to take a more holistic approach by exploring the emotional causes – as well as bodily symptoms – when making a diagnosis.

Things are only heavy when you hold them. To walk through life more lightly, practice letting go as often as possible.

The essence of being present is a feeling of being *as one with life*, and the only prerequisite for this is to travel as lightly as possible, a lightness that comes through a deliberate and disciplined approach to letting go. So let go of those outmoded beliefs, stories and resentments you have (you know which ones they are – the ones that cause you either emotional or physical pain, or both). Or if you find it too hard to let go, then at the very least, you must try to loosen your grip because it's this gripping, this clinging, that pulls you out of the present and into pain.

Frequently, it's the little things we need to constantly let go of in order to create a more harmonious life – letting go of a negative thought we're holding about what someone said to us, letting go of the tension from a recent argument, or letting go of the need to be right. These situations arise every day, and one of the arts of living is to look at each of these situations and be able to say to yourself, 'Great! Here's another chance to let go', and simply view it as part of your practice.

Once you change the pattern of having to hold onto the little things, you'll become excited about the possibility of letting go of bigger things, such as ingrained thinking habits and negative self-talk. Little by little, you'll find yourself moving away from past hurts and towards present harmony, and it will begin to dawn on you that you don't need to hold onto anything to be happy. It's in the letting go that you find your true freedom.

Freedom Phrase: 'Let go. Let be. Let in.'

Also see: Shed the Armour – page 70

And try this practice: Let It Go – page 111

Love Yourself.

'If you have love you will do all things well.'
Thomas Merton, Writer & Mystic

Everyone on this planet has the desire to experience love. From the moment we're born right up until the moment we die, being connected to (or disconnected from) love is always the core theme of our life, lying at the root of just about every thought we think, every feeling we experience, every action we take. How we feel within ourselves and how we feel about others at any given time is directly proportional to the amount of self-love we are able to experience.

To the extent you are absorbed by your past (or possible future), you may miss out on the benefits of this vital connection. Overindulgence in thinking or worrying creates a separation between your thoughts and your feelings, making it harder to experience 'heartfelt' emotion and opening up a void inside you.

Some will attempt to fill the void with substitutes: one night stands, drugs, junk food – anything to distract themselves from the fact that they have become alienated from their authentic loving natures. These poor substitutes only serve to distance us further from our desire to experience the *completeness* of self-love.

For those who have been cut off from love, perhaps through childhood trauma, the desire to *have* love can turn into an obsession. When love is regarded as something to be possessed, it creates pain because it is also then able to be lost. This simple principle lies at the core of most jealously, mistrust and other relationship dysfunctions. After all, you cannot *have* love – you can only *be* in love.

Love is a state of *being*; it is only active in and can only exist in the present moment.

In its purest form, love is a feeling of freedom, of having a deep sense of connection to everything as it stands in the moment. It cannot be found by searching outside of ourselves; it can only be discovered and nurtured from the *inside*. It's no coincidence that those who spend their lives striving for happiness also have trouble experiencing love; the search for happiness is actually the search for love – a love of yourself and then a love of the world around you.

It's said that 'love is blind', not necessarily blind to reality, but oblivious to judgment and discrimination. When we're in love, we look for (and see) the best in everybody and everything. If you've ever had the occasion to be near new lovers, you'll know that it's hard not to be affected by their lightness of being and zest for life. It's contagious. While it's easy to believe that the happy couple are in love with *each other*, in reality their union has simply allowed them to openly express the love that is already within them. It could be said that they are in love with themselves, *together*.

Moving closer to self-love starts by letting go of the past, of the hurt that you're carrying. If you don't let go, you will always be offering your love to others from a position of pain; you'll *need* their love and you will want something in return. True love cannot be conditional; it requires trust and faith, most of all in yourself.

Instead of seeking love, start investing in yourself. Schedule time for activities that make you feel connected and happy, be they solitary (bush walking, swimming, etc.) or more social in nature (card games, sports, etc.). These activities help you to reconnect with the present and create more personal fulfilment in your life; these are the environmental conditions that nurture self-love.

You may find, as you begin to open the door to your intrinsic beauty and value, that it initially evokes a feeling of loss and sadness – perhaps even moving you to tears. If this happens, take it as a good sign; your trapped emotions have seen an opening and seeking release. Find a quiet place to unburden yourself of the hurt you are carrying. Congratulate yourself on clearing some of the path required so that more love may shine *through* you.

The gateway to (re)discovering the love that you are lies right here in the present moment. Nurture this moment and you will nurture and grow your loving nature, which in turn will attract more loving people and circumstances into your life.

Freedom Phrase: 'I love myself.'

Also see: Come Home – page 52

And try this practice: Follow Your Bliss – page 91

Be Quiet.

'Either go and be with what you are thinking about, or be here. Don't try to be in two places.'
Barry Long, Spiritual Teacher, Writer, Former Australian Press Secretary

Typically, when two people have a conversation today, there are actually *three* conversations going on; the one being had together and a separate one in the minds of each person. Few have the presence of mind necessary to listen to another person completely without drifting off into thought or judgment, whether it is thinking about how the conversation relates to your own experience (the past), or thinking about what you would like to say next (the future). It's a product of the mind-centric world that we live in; a world where everything must be prioritised, categorised, labelled and have its worth assessed.

When meeting a person of importance, influence or stature, you may find yourself weighing up your worth verses theirs. Questions run through the back of your mind: 'Do they have more than me?' and 'What do I have that can compare or impress them?' When you do interact, it's likely you'll find your attention focused on how you are coming across – or how to present yourself in the best light – rather than focusing your attention on them and their value as a fellow human being. At best, you might come off as slightly disingenuous, and at worst, it may seem incongruous and wooden, the opposite of what you'd like.

At best, your attention is only *partially* focused on the conversation, with the remainder directed towards your thoughts about it. When you remove yourself from the conversation in this way, you lose your spontaneity (to be spontaneous, you must be present), you limit the inherent potential for new ideas to spark, and you limit the energy required to fully engage in the exchange. The more your attention wavers, the more you stymie the creative and bonding potential within the interaction.

The obvious solution is to try and become less preoccupied with yourself and redirect your focus 100% onto the other. Try to *listen from nothing*, which is the practice of switching off – or at least turning down the volume on – the conversation in your head. A good way to do this is to bring to mind a blank sheet of paper or an empty canvass just before you enter the conversation, to 'clear the slate' so to speak.

Byconsciouslyclearingoutyourjudgementsandassumptionsbeforeyouengageinconversation, you are able to be more present and connect more deeply.

This can be quite challenging, as we typically bring a lot of baggage into our day-to-day conversations, whether they be with friends, colleagues or strangers. We all have experienced dialogue that follows the same pattern, where the predetermined beliefs and judgements of each party (think parents or ex-partners) lead to a predictable outcome – and often not a happy one. When you can listen from nothing, the way you receive communication changes, with new information being assessed for its own intrinsic value and interest.

The more you can let go of the need to imprint yourself on the interaction, the easier it will be. While this does not guarantee that your companion will do the same, it does bring *your* awareness and concentration into the present and promotes a far more authentic conversation. By removing the need to pre-empt, better, or position yourself, you open up your attention and enhance your ability to read the tonality and subtext inherent in the conversation. You begin to understand, interpret and respond to ideas, comments and statements more effectively and fluidly by following the spontaneous flow of the conversation. This mindful awareness allows for the creation of ideas and opportunities that neither of you may have previously thought possible.

Perhaps more than this, you are now being true to both yourself and those you engage in conversation; you're not having a separate discussion from the one happening in real time. You are invested right here in the present, where the greatest ideas, solutions and friendships are always generated.

Freedom Phrase: 'Listen from nothing.'

Also see: See the Everyday Gurus – page 72

And try this practice: Be in the Conversation – page 95

Take Action.

'First say to yourself what you would be; and then do what you have to do.'
Epictetus, Greek Philosopher, Former Slave

The relationship between *thought* and *action* is one that most people never consider – even though it lies at the root of much of our mental stress and discord. Just as we perceive our mind and body as separate, we tend to segregate our thoughts and actions in the same way. It is the disconnect between what we are *thinking* and what we are (or are not) *doing* about our thoughts that causes so many problems in our lives..

Your thoughts crave physical expression; they exist so that you can take considered and decisive action. When thought is followed by action, it creates change and growth. This is healthy. If you're thinking about what you need to do with an *intention* of taking action on it, it means your mind and body are in alignment. If you then act on the thought, you release the thought-energy.

But some would prefer to think about things (worrying about their own situation or gossiping about others) and *not* take any action. They spend their time thinking and talking about things they have *no intention* of doing or pursuing, which creates an atmosphere full of high emotion and blocked energy, which runs at odds with the natural order of life, which is – to *think*, then *do*.

Worrying about a problem or issue does nothing to help solve it – it only exacerbates and perpetuates the issue, creating a climate of disempowerment and helplessness. Have you ever lain awake at night worrying about your finances, your relationship, your health or job security? Has the worrying itself *ever* helped resolve these issues? It's unlikely. Fear prevents you from taking the necessary steps to address and solve these problems. Fear has a paralysing effect on your ability to act and keeps you stuck in the past. To take action, you must be willing and prepared to overcome the fear of change.

For example, if you find yourself in an unfulfilling job, you have two options: either to accept the situation as it stands, (which many will do out of fear of not having any immediate alternative) or take action towards changing the situation. If, out of fear, you procrastinate on making any decision to act, then you must also be prepared to accept your dissatisfaction with the way things are and the notion of things improving. Continuing to think (or worry) about it will not only bring you more discomfort and pain, but also negatively affect your health and wellbeing.

Fear keeps you stuck in the past, but *action* brings you back into the present.

Action always exists in the present moment. When you take action, it's always in the now – even if the motivation driving the action comes from the past or future. This is why you often feel so relieved when you finally 'speak up' or do something bold that you've been putting off out of fear. That's not to say that taking action immediately makes things easier or better; in fact, sometimes it's quite the opposite! But the energy you get from taking action allows you to cope with any short-term discomfort and helps you to develop your *thought-action* muscle so you can take more control of your life.

There is no point in allowing thoughts to dominate your mind unless you have the intention and a plan to do something about them. Either *think* then *do*; or if you're not prepared to do anything, then *let go of the thought*. Make a decision. Put the time aside, sit down and get started; tell you best friend, 'No', speak to your partner, write that letter, talk to the boss, buy that guitar you've always wanted – just DO something!

Action is the gateway to your personal evolution and inner-state management; the faster you can think, act and learn, the faster you will evolve and the happier you will become.

Freedom Phrase: 'Take action or *let go of the thought*.'

Also see: Stop Overthinking – page 35

And try this practice: Let It Go – page 111

Come Home.

'*Wherever you go, there you are.*'
The Brady Bunch Movie

So just what does it mean to be *at home*?

For most, home is the place where their own room or bed is, or where their mail is delivered, or where their family resides. Home is seen as the place we go (or return) to when we want to feel secure, a place where we can remove the protective armour donned throughout the day, a place where we can just relax and *be* ourselves. Home is a place where we find it easy to be present.

For many, this one location is the *only* place they will allow themselves to experience serenity. Everywhere else, no matter how luxurious or comfortable, just doesn't feel like home and, because they don't feel the safety of home, some part of them is always on guard. It is this discomfort, this disquiet, that creates a barrier to accepting and appreciating the moment as it stands. It keeps you in your head and out of the present moment, making it impossible to feel connected, joyous and light.

An essential aspect of feeling of genuinely alive is the ability to experience the serenity of *home* when you are in new and different environments. While some degree of apprehension is natural in strange surroundings, being able to quiet your mind and accept the newness of your situation helps keep you centred and adds more depth to your experience. The bonus is that, when *you* feel at home, you make *others* feel at home too, opening up the possibility for more warmth, generosity and connection for everyone.

Wheneveryouareabletomakepeacewithyourenvironmentandjust*beyourself*,youareessentially at home.

When you find yourself in a situation or place that makes you feel uncomfortable or like an outsider, ask yourself, 'Where is my attention?' If you are focused on what is strange or different, you are actively separating yourself from the environment, keeping yourself in your head, and out of the present moment. While this fear state exists only in your mind, it is (often unconsciously) communicated non-verbally to others, further exacerbating your discomfort, and that of those around you.

To start moving past the unease or nervousness of new or strange situations, look for what is familiar as this will help you put yourself at ease. Take a slow, deep belly breath, as this will help release some of the tension. After all, home is simply your inner state of peace and presence that you can call on anytime. Say to yourself, 'Home is always within me', as this will remind you that your inner state is always within your control and that nothing can reach or harm you there unless you allow it to. It is your thinking that is making you uncomfortable and often *not* the environment.

But what of those times when you are at home, but you *still* feel insecure – when you struggle to feel comfortable or relaxed even when within your own four walls? Unfortunately, the restless discontent so commonly associated with modern living is often carried into our home environment and can disrupt even our most sacred zones.

To counter this, it is important to take time out to manage your state *before* distracting yourself with food, TV or Facebook. Look for ways to still your mind and create comfort, perhaps by having a bath, listening to your favourite music – or even making your own! You may prefer to go out for a walk or run. Whatever you do, your intention should be to nurture yourself, so you can connect to the present and once again feel centred and at peace.

Freedom Phrase: 'Always at home.'

Also see: Look for the Like – page 62

And try this practice: Just Breathe – page 81

Choose It.

'Work is love made visible.'
Kahlil Gibran, Persian Poet, Artist, Rebel

In prosperous societies, where increasing wealth provides us with more leisure opportunities, it's easy to form the view that work is a *necessary evil*, something to be suffered through or, if at all possible, to be avoided completely. Many dream of – and spend a lot of money on – winning the lottery so they can give up work and live a life of leisure. But this is often just a pipedream, an escapist fantasy that helps to take some of the sting out of the way that many have chosen to live their lives.

The American poet Henry David Thoreau summed this up when he wrote that many people 'lead lives of quiet desperation', going through the motions every day, but never really feeling fulfilled. In this detached state, once fun-loving, hopeful people become increasingly numb, resigning themselves to just *getting on with it*, the idea of experiencing a real connection – both within themselves and with others – given up in favour of a smaller, but seemingly safer, world. This mode of existence inevitably leads to seeking out other ways to experience this sense of belonging, including indulging in petty gossip or hitting the pub for happy hour after work.

In this *alienated* perspective, an ongoing and underlying dissatisfaction exists with the present moment. Rather than being able to appreciate what is good about your situation, you can only see what's *wrong* with it. When you're alienated from what you do day-to-day, it's easy to feel like you're not acting of your own free will, but rather being *acted upon* by forces beyond your control. You may see your boss as an evil overlord, working you like a slave; or perhaps, you are driven by your own compulsive need to compete and prove yourself. Either way, you feel like you are only doing what you *have to* do and someone else is to blame for your situation.

Escape from this debilitating mindset is simple – but not easy. You must be able to *choose* what it is that you are doing, whether it be a shitty job, late-night study or tedious household chores. You must learn to *accept* where you are in your life and stop all the resistance and blame, as only then will you release your grip on what 'should be' and begin to align once again to 'what is'. This may sound counter-intuitive; after all, who in their right mind would choose to do any of these things?

You would.

You chose to do the things that you hate, just as you chose to do the things that you love. Your life has been shaped as a result of exercising your own free will. You have always had the option of choosing *not* to do these things, as long as you were prepared to deal with the consequences (be it an upset boss, failing grades or an untidy house). You chose to do them because you were likely trying to improve your life situation – or at least make the best of the options you saw as available to you. Ultimately, the choice has *always* been yours.

A sense of empowerment is experienced with the realisation that much of your life is the sum of all the choices you have made. By accepting this notion, you can release some of the mental resistance and allow the creative and vital energy to flow back into your life. You will stop feeling like someone else is in control of your life and you will start to take back the reigns and accept responsibility for the choices you have made that have landed you here.

By choosing your situation you create acceptance and with acceptance comes presence.

Choosing to accept your situation is an important first step, giving you a reprieve to regather your energy and use this to assess your situation. Ask yourself important questions, such as, 'What do I really want?' and 'If I died tomorrow, what would I regret *not* doing most?' When you are ready to ask these questions, you are ready to hear the answers. Take swift action on any intuitive ideas that come to you to initiate the momentum of change. Then, slowly and gently start to track to a new path, to a life that allows you to feel more present, more connected and more valuable.

Freedom Phrase: 'I choose this.'

Also see: Evolve – page 58

And try this practice: Control the Controllable – page 109

Find Your Flow.

'You were born with wings; why do you prefer to crawl through life?'
Rumi

Whether you are someone who loves what you do for a living or someone who sees work more as a 'means to an end', there have likely been times when you have become so completely absorbed in your work that time seemed to fly by and it actually became *fun*. When you hit this 'zone' all that seems to matter is the task that you are focused on doing, you are able to quieten the mental noise and experience that unmistakable surge of positive energy that is created when 100% of your attention is directed into the now.

'When an activity is thoroughly engrossing, there is not enough attention left over to allow a person to consider either the past or the future,' says Dr Mihaly Csikszentmihalyi, a noted positive psychologist and nicknamed the 'Father of Flow'. In his book *Flow: The Psychology of Optimal Experience*, Dr Csikszentmihalyi describes 'flow' as 'being completely involved in an activity for its own sake. The ego falls away. Time flies. Every action, movement, and thought follows inevitably from the previous one…your whole being is involved, and you're using your skills to the utmost.'

In moments of *flow*, you are profoundly present.

Dr Csikszentmihalyi studied these 'optimal experiences', and his research has turned up something very interesting. He found that optimal experiences (or flow) states were reported more frequently by his test subjects when they were at work rather than at leisure. This ran at odds with the general notion that we derive more satisfaction when we are *not* at work! He refers to this counter-intuitive finding as the *Paradox of Work*. The fact is that, while work tends to get a bad rap, we actually report being happier and more engaged when we are engrossed in productive work activity over many of our (sometimes rather sedentary) leisure-time activities.

Put simply, flow is a state of *active presence*. It can occur in all sorts of places and doing all sorts of things including, household chores, preparing meals – even just when walking down the street. It occurs whenever your mind temporarily coalesces with your action, and you are instantly rewarded with a burst of joyous energy (and probably dopamine). What's more, when you are in the flow state, you tend to inspire the interest and attention of others. Flow is not only fun – it's also acts like a magnet. Just by pouring yourself into the things you love to do, you unwittingly draw others into your circle of presence.

Think about how we love to watch the best players, musicians and singers performing; it's a mesmerising force that energises both the performer and the observer simultaneously. This is also one of the reasons we love sport so much. Watching or participating in a closely contested match can be exhilarating, sweeping us deeply into the moment and forming a strong emotional bond between the players and the spectators. This bond is forged by all parties relinquishing their hold on the past and future and surrendering to the moment.

You have opportunities to experience flow every day, but you have to be alert to them. Start by noticing those moments when you are working and experience a sense of timelessness or ease, and then step back a little. How are you feeling inside? What are you doing that makes it feel so good? The more you become aware of those times when you are in flow, the better you can become at managing it. Soon you will start directing more of your efforts towards those activities that make you feel flow in, and spending less time with those that don't. By doing this, you take a step towards a freedom of spirit that will help to rejuvenate you and shine a light for others to follow.

Freedom Phrase: 'Keep stepping towards your flow.'

Also see: Lead with Intention – page 37

And try this practice: Follow Your Bliss – page 91

Evolve.

'A tree either grows or decays; it does not ever stand still.'
Unknown

Nothing living stands still in this world – unless it's on the tipping point of stagnation and decay. The process of evolution is one of continual growth until, either by circumstance or design, the regression back to the earth begins. The flower is busy being a flower, right up until the moment it starts to wither and die. While it is living, however, the flower is *very much* alive and always pushing skyward.

Yet, in stark contradiction to these natural laws, many people feel that they can stop learning, stop growing, stop changing – and somehow miraculously suffer no side effects. Some may feel they have already learned, accomplished or experienced enough. Others just give up. When this happens the urge to grow and evolve is unwittingly relinquished, our health and happiness suffers, and the downward slide towards stagnation commences.

When we stop challenging ourselves, stop learning and start resisting change, our attitudes harden, and we become more rigid and less open, distancing ourselves both from the moment we're in and from the people around us. It's not a case of being old. It's not a case of being unwell. It's a case of being *scared*. Fear holds us back. Fear keeps us stuck to the past, and the more we hold on, the more we suffer.

If you are to be present, if you are to flourish, you must consciously turn towards change and growth.

Just as a tree will grow stronger when buffeted by the winds, a certain amount of resistance or pressure is necessary for our development, both physically and mentally. Our bodies respond to resistance training by becoming stronger and more enduring. Our minds respond to mental resistance and challenges by becoming more agile and resourceful. We all need at least some resistance to be happy and fulfilled – but how much is the *right* amount?

Too much resistance (or stress), whether it is physical or mental, will eventually overwhelm us and potentially lead to breakdown; too little resistance and our bodies will weaken, our minds becoming blunt. The trick is to find the sweet spot, a place where there's just enough challenge to keep you engaged and growing, but not so much that you feel overwhelmed and anxious. This creates something called 'eustress', a healthy form of stress that helps to keep your senses sharp.

If you're feeling bored and disengaged with your work you have two options; you can either start looking for other more stimulating work (which many won't do out of fear of change) or you can find more ways to up the ante: ask the boss for a new project, develop a new strategy or start mentoring others. Conversely, if you feel overwhelmed by what's on your plate, rather than suffering in silence (or potentially quitting), look for ways to dial back the pressure, perhaps getting further training, mentoring or support. In each instance, the key to getting back in balance is recognizing the issue and then taking positive action toward the change you want or need.

Your emotions provide you with a simple but powerful navigational tool to help manage this balance; if you are feeling bored or depressed, this signals it's time to step out of your comfort zone and challenge yourself with something new. If you are feeling stressed out or highly anxious, this signals you should look for ways to alleviate some of the pressure, either through additional support or by stepping down the challenge. Either way, it's important that you proactively manage your growth in order to stay in the sweet spot.

Get this right and you will return to feeling connected, productive and in alignment with your true nature.

Freedom Phrase: 'A tree either grows or decays – it does not stand still.'

Also see: Take Action – page 50

And try this practice: Change the Script – page 113

Serve.

It's said that we make a *living* by what we get, but we make a *life* by what we give. Yet, in our mad scramble to become 'successful', our focus and intention has moved from helping *others* to helping *ourselves* – to getting rather than giving. We have become so preoccupied with accumulating possessions and wealth that we seem to have forgotten the premise that all work is founded on: to further the welfare of our community and fellow man.

Environmentalist and author David Orr captures this concept beautifully in this excerpt from his book *Earth in Mind*: 'The plain fact is that the planet does not need more "successful people". But it does desperately need more peacemakers, healers, restorers, storytellers and lovers of all kinds. It needs people to live well in their places. It needs people of moral courage willing to join the fight to make the world habitable and humane. And these qualities have little to do with success as our culture has defined it.'

When you grow up in a culture where to *have* more is to *be* more, you can become consumed with thoughts of your own personal advancement, on achieving more fame, status or income. Your head gets so far up in the clouds that you forget about how much you are needed back down here on earth. You start seeing yourself as the centre of your own universe, with everything else being assessed in terms of its relationship to you. This self-directed focus not only separates you from the moment, but also separates you *from your humanity*, feeding your ego and only fuelling further self-centred, and often self-destructive, behaviour.

This state of being is fundamentally broken. Ultimately, it is always your *contribution* that determines your value to society. The more you contribute, the more goodwill, reciprocity (and income) you will generate in return. Nowhere can this model be more starkly noted than in the business community. Businesses (and their directors) that are in it for the short-term gain (think HIH or Enron) often fail spectacularly, while those that exist to serve and create value (think Google, Southwest Airlines and Virgin) seem to move from strength to strength.

Service to others is the foundation of any good friendship, marriage, working relationship or business. The desire to act selflessly for the betterment of others unites us and creates harmony in our world. If you are restless or dissatisfied with your life, perhaps it's worth asking whom you have been serving lately. Is your attention focused on yourself or others? By shifting the spotlight onto others, you'll start to feel better almost immediately. Indeed, there is now a growing pool of evidence to suggest that being involved in some type of community service activity helps to alleviate the symptoms of people suffering from depression.

When you serve others unconditionally, you give up your ego, release your grip on time, and become present.

Start with the small offerings; cook a surprise dinner for your partner or friend, sit down with your kids and really get interested in what they are doing, or go above and beyond to look after one of your customers. Notice how you feel each time you do this; notice the positive energy created both within yourself and within others. But please don't do it with the expectation of reciprocation – the pay-off is how you feel when you give yourself to the task unconditionally. You can never get less through giving.

You may even choose to take bolder steps, such as volunteering in a charitable organisation or perhaps even travelling overseas to help in an orphanage for a time. These experiences can be life-changing and can offer a completely fresh perspective on what it means to be human in this time of rapid progress and change.

However you may choose to approach it, make being of service part of your life's mission. By giving freely of yourself, you open the door to living more in the moment, as well as kick-starting a virtuous cycle of contribution that makes you feel great and helps heal the world around you.

Freedom Phrase: 'Find yourself by losing yourself in service to others.'

Also see: Simplify – page 39

And try this practice: Be in the Conversation – page 95

Look for the Like.

'Being separate is an illusion, inevitably brought about by our entry into the physical world of matter.'
Rainer Taeni, Rebirthing Coach, Love Expert

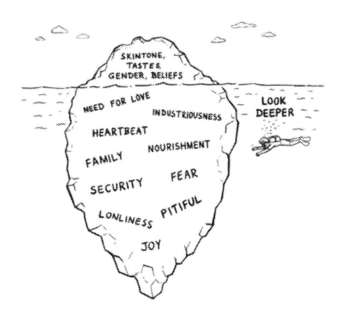

Humans are prolific *labellers*, and we assess and categorise everything we come across according to the current catalogue of files stored within our cerebral hard drives. If an object or situation is known to us, or fits a previous pattern, we are comfortable with it. But when faced with something new or different (unfamiliar clothing, accents, music, smells, etc.), we may experience discomfort up until the time that we have properly identified it. If a quick label for it is not available to us it, we will often choose to separate ourselves from it and even regard it with suspicion or judge it harshly, until some familiarly is gained.

When in unfamiliar territory, it is a natural tendency to operate from a *defensive* position, one in which we look for ways to feel superior to – or at least on par with – others, and where we are forever assessing our self-worth against those around us. If they don't dress as smartly or speak the same, we are quick to attach unflattering labels. If they seem stronger, more capable or confident, we may look for areas to criticise (either silently to ourselves or verbally to others) in order to bring them down a peg or two to make up for the fact that we feel threatened.

We live in a culture where it is deemed acceptable to spend hours gossiping about the size, dress sense or behaviour of others, to take pleasure in belittling and bullying in order to garner short-lived attention and power. This temptation to judge and diminish others as a way to elevate our own status can be hard to resist, and especially so when our politicians, the supposed leaders of our society, stray from the agenda and resort to taking personal pot-shots at each other.

Rather than focusing on the differences and alienating yourself, instead put your attention on what you have in common, the qualities (or even quirks) you share with those around you. Commonalities such as the need for love and acceptance, or the fact you love your mothers, or even that you like the same sport or football team. This shift in attention reduces the divide between you and others, creating the opportunity for more open, spontaneous interaction. Sure, recognize and discuss the differences, but do not make them the basis of your evaluation – see the common first.

To be present in new or strange situations, look for the qualities that unite you – not what separates you.

By adopting this uniting perspective, you will increase your sense of connectedness and belonging. When you become aware of your judgement of others, you become free to let go of the fear of not *being enough* or not fitting in, for this is where much of your stress and resistance emanates from. It's this fear that keeps us from being present, open hearted and being all we can be.

The next time you find yourself judging others, ask yourself, 'What am I threatened by?' Maybe it's that *you* don't feel strong, smart or successful enough. Perhaps you feel envious of the other because they have something you aspire to have yourself, be it a swept-up car or great looking partner. Noticing this is a very positive step! Once you realize that the separation between yourself and others is actually *your own feelings reflected onto them* – you can start taking action towards making changes in your life. You may even find that the person (or people), you have been judging so harshly are the same ones who can help you take the next step in your own personal evolution.

When you judge others, it is not because of a lack within them – it is a lack within you. Instead, look for something about the person or people being judged that you can relate to or appreciate. You might find they have a nice smile or quit wit. If nothing else, they are loved by *someone*, so look at them as being loveable.

Discipline yourself to look for sameness over differences, and you'll create a sense of ease and presence within yourself, enabling you to connect more easily with the people around you.

Freedom Phrase: 'What I see in others is a reflection of myself.'

Also see: Love Yourself – page 46

And try this practice: Empowering Affirmations – page 99

Feel it.

'A feeling is an energetic connection with the present… an emotion is an energetic tie to the past.'
Rainer Taeni, Rebirthing Coach, Love Expert

In the developing world, we have become so obsessed with thinking that we tend to override our body's natural signals telling us how we feel (we'd rather pop a pill than take the time to explore what is going on within us). When this is done repeatedly the feeling remains unexpressed and locked within us as an emotional disturbance within our body (the Latin root verb of emotion is *emovere*, meaning 'move out'). This can lead to nervous disorders and even weaken our immune system.

The *feeling* has now become an *emotion*, a bundle of energy that has been swallowed back down and kept in the body rather than being expressed. Many see the words *feelings* and *emotions* as interchangeable – but there is an importance difference that will help you to rejuvenate and reset your connection with the moment.

Feelings are bodily sensations brought about by changes in our electromagnetic energy; they play a vital role in guiding our responses and actions. Feelings are often experienced in the abdomen (where your 'gut brain' is located), and lie at the root of your intuition, giving you subtle (and sometimes not so subtle) physical

sensations that help you to make decisions. Feelings are created in the *present* and, unless stymied for some reason, tend to seek physical expression, washing through and over you before extinguishing themselves.

Expressing how you feel is healthy and helps you to deal with change (anxiety), cope with conflict (anger) and loss (sadness), as well as embrace celebration (joy). Being in touch with your feelings is one of the vital ingredients to living a joyous and connected life. It's your feelings that keep you tapped into your source energy and feeling alive. Women tend to be better calibrated for this than men and are able to recognize the physical cues and more easily attach words to their feelings (sometimes to the chagrin of the men in their lives!).

Emotions represent feelings that have been generated *in the past*, perhaps due to childhood experiences that, for whatever reason, were unable to be expressed at the time. These stymied thoughts – and feelings fuelling them – then lie hidden in the subconscious, subtly but continually influencing one's thoughts and behaviour. Emotions are triggered *first* by the mind and *then* are felt by the body, whereas feelings are experienced simultaneously in the mind *and* body, and perform a cleansing function (think about how refreshing it was the last time you had a good cry or punched out your anger in a bag).

If someone was coming at you with a knife, most likely you would *feel* fear, and both your mind and body would respond instantaneously with one of the three F's (fight/ flight/freeze) impulses. Your heart rate would increase, adrenaline would rush through your body and your digestion would be temporarily suspended (or evacuated). Here, the feeling of fear – and the bodily changes it brings with it – serves as a means for you to either defend yourself…or lighten the load and hightail it out of there!

Yet you may have felt this same type of physical reaction to fear when called on to speak in front of a group – even though your life was not in danger. This is the *emotion* of fear; a fear first created by the mind, in turn activating a feeling stored in the body – perhaps a feeling of past embarrassment, failure or general insecurity which was left unexpressed.

To begin to lighten the load you must start by paying close attention to what you feel.

It's important to ask yourself regularly, '*What* am I feeling right now?' Slow down for a second and check your body; notice the physical sensations, perhaps a tightness in the tummy, a sharp pain in the temple or a flushed feeling in the cheeks. Try not to ask yourself, '*How* am I feeling?', as the word 'How' invites your mind to make an assessment of your state, rather than checking in with your body directly – which will always be honest with you. Instead ask '*What* am I feeling?'

Your feelings are there to help you navigate through life and therefore need to be befriended rather than shunned or buried. Their role could be summed up being as your GPS map towards a positive life and therefore it's a good idea to adhere to them. Emotions stemming from past experiences often bring with them feelings of anguish and pain. They can lead you off your path and into the weeds so it's important to identify the fork in the road and make a conscious effort to stay on track.

THE PRESENT.

When you start to bring awareness to the tide of your underlying thoughts and emotions, you'll begin to notice that the way you perceive others is often a reflection of what you are feeling yourself. If are carrying anger, you will experience more angry people. If you are feeling negative, you will see what's wrong with everyone, no matter how saintly they may be.

Use your judgement of others as a prompt to go inside and identify the thoughts that are occupying your mind. It is these thoughts that are creating the emotion, and ultimately shaping your *life experience*. Make a commitment to challenge these thoughts (or stories) in order to regain your presence of mind. Don't allow your unchecked thinking to keep emotion spiralling around inside of you. Change it. Release it. Express it.

But don't stop feeling.

Freedom Phrase: Ask '*What* am I feeling?' Not '*How* am I feeling?'

Also see: Shield Your State – page 33

And try this practice: Body Scan – page 103

Lose the Ego.

'Between stimulus and response there is a space.
In that space is our power to choose our response.
In our response lies our growth and our freedom.'
Viktor E. Frankl, MD, PhD, Author, WWII Concentration Camp survivor

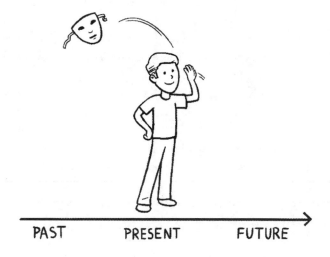

PAST   PRESENT   FUTURE

So much of the emotional pain inflicted in our world arises from our defensive reactions towards others. While outwardly we may like to portray ourselves as centred and self-assured, this is often just a mask. It may only take one poorly timed comment, or slight inconvenience, for us to lose our cool or lash out, betraying our calm facade and opening a window into our *real* inner state.

It's said that 'hurt people *hurt* people'. Those who carry hurt or pain will often act in a way (intentionally or otherwise) that causes harm to others when their ego (or sense of self) feels threatened. Just as only a small proportion of an iceberg is visible above the sea with the bulk lying hidden beneath the surface, our egoic reactions are often the tip of a much larger emotional iceberg hidden deep within us.

In his powerful book *The Power of Now*, Eckhart Tolle refers to this invisible (and dangerous) bundle of unexpressed emotion as the 'pain-body', saying: 'The pain-body wants to survive, just like every other entity in existence, and it can only survive if it gets you to unconsciously identify with it. It can then rise up, take you over, become you, and live through you.' He goes onto say that to sustain itself, the pain body must feed on more pain and it will create anger, grief and emotional drama in order to do this.

THE PRESENT.

It's likely that you do not see your ego (or pain body) as being separate from you, and this is because it is so ingrained that you can only view it as part of yourself. Yet all ego is fictitious; it is created by you as a way of coping with the world you entered into and now must survive in. When you say things such as, 'I'm shy' or I'm outgoing', or even, 'I'm terrible with names', this is you reinforcing an identity that you have come to know yourself as. And because this is the image you have developed for identity, you will protect it from any perceived attack with the same vigour as you would protect yourself from a physical attack.

Your ego developed when you were young and was the result of your response to emotionally challenging (as well as emotionally fulfilling) situations. Perhaps, as a child, you were left to cry when you yearned for comforting, leaving you to develop the notion that 'When I'm upset, no one cares', and therefore 'I have to fend for myself.' Or maybe you found it hard to get noticed by busy working parents who had other kids to attend to and developed an idea that 'I need to perform to be liked', and then, 'I need to be liked to be worthwhile.' Conversely, you may have been praised along every step of your childhood, and now feel unrealistically invincible and carry an overinflated sense of entitlement.

While it may have started innocently enough, once these seeds of belief, however misinformed, were planted, they took root through repetitive thinking until the thoughts became so ingrained in you that they became indistinguishable from what you consider to be your personality. You learned to believe that you *are* the thoughts you had as a child, and even as an adult, you continue to apply the same defensive strategies that you learned in your formative years – often to a counterproductive effect.

When you're in the grip of ego, your feelings and actions are directed by your past experience, alienating you from the present.

Thankfully, those with higher levels of empathy towards you, perhaps dear friends or loving parents, still manage to see past your pain body, knowing that this is simply a cover for unresolved insecurities and feelings that lie deep within you. They instinctively know that these strong reactions really have little to do with the present situation, but are linked to a past hurt or fear, so they handle you with care. We come to truly love and depend on these people because they allow us to see ourselves through their eyes as lovable, worthy individuals.

If you're ready to gain more control over your conditioned self, start noticing when you have a strong emotional reaction to a situation. Ask yourself, 'Is this appropriate to *this* situation, or am I bringing something else to it?', or 'Does this reaction fit the situation, or is this my pain body speaking?' Step back for a moment to assess the true feeling that's rising up from inside you. Anger? Sadness? Loss? Try to define it. What thought or memory is associated with this feeling? Don't try to force an answer; just ponder it for a moment and then allow it to settle. Be gentle with yourself.

As you shine light into the dark corners where your past hurt is lurking, the connection between your present situation and your past pain becomes more apparent and easier to tease out. With practice and patience, you'll develop more spontaneous and authentic connections with yourself and others, as well as an ability to enjoy the present moment as it stands and not having to change or control it. When you appreciate things as they are, without being overshadowed by past hurts, you experience freedom. Your actions are no longer being dictated by the past, and you are free to create the next chapter of your life right here, in the infinite opportunity of the present moment.

Freedom Phrase: 'It's impossible to inhale new air until you exhale the old'

Also see: Challenge the Story – page 41

And try this practice: Let It Go – page 111

Shed the Armour.

'If you want to see what your body will be like tomorrow, look at your thoughts today.'
Deepak Chopra, Author, Alternative Health Advocate, Owner of Virgin Comics

Your thoughts have an instant impact on your body. If you perceive a situation to be safe, your body operates in its natural present state. But if a situation is perceived to be threatening – either to your psyche or your physical body – your body chemistry changes immediately as your body protects itself, as if going into battle.

Just as two people may be screaming on the same roller coaster for completely different reasons (one out of joy and one from sheer *terror*), two people may look out the very same window with one seeing the world as exciting, inviting and accepting, and the other seeing it as cold and foreboding...even terrifying.

When you experience fear (either real or imagined), your innate protective response is to tense your muscles and hold your breath – this is known as *armouring*. Over time and through constant repetition, this unconscious reaction will eventually leave a physical imprint on your body. Shallow breathing born of fear may create or exacerbate conditions such as asthma or speech impediments. A reoccurring sore back or neck may be connected to unexpressed feelings of anger or frustration. Mysterious digestive disorders can also be explained by the armouring of the gut, many times a result of chronic fear or high anxiety. Left unchecked, armouring can become so chronic that it may lead to serious conditions requiring hospitalisation, even surgery.

The trigger responsible for armouring your body are the thoughts you entertain about a particular situation. These are often derived from your childhood interpretation of events, and your body's still armouring itself in order to protect you. While this is a natural response – and perhaps unavoidable – the result is negative energy from the past being stored in your body, making it hard for you to relax.

But even if we have armoured ourselves over many years, the cells in our bodies have the ability to regenerate, allowing the body to realign. Dr Deepak Chopra believes that we hold onto our feelings and emotions even down to a cellular level. Our cells retain the emotional energy that passes through our organs, muscles and tissues, and a 'cellular memory' develops. The cells of the body lose their memory of wholeness and connectedness to the rest of the body, and the cells begin to 'react randomly, causing havoc and destruction' when we allow negative emotions to go unexamined. Even after a cell regenerates, 'phantom memories' exist and are transferred to the new cells. This, says Chopra, is the source of *all* disease and illness.

How can we remove this emotional armour so that we can clear and release our repressed feelings and emotions? There's no doubt that the help of a qualified counsellor or therapist can be effective, as they can work with you to identify, and potentially resolve, your buried emotional pain. But even without the help of a therapist, you can start working on loosening the grip that these emotional imprints have on you.

Start by noticing where you most often feel tension or physical pain. It may be something that has bothered you for years, but no one's been able to help you get to the root of the issue. What exactly is that condition or weakness? See if you can find words to describe the pain or discomfort, like heat, tension, tingling, weakness, throbbing, tight, etc. You might also want to pay attention to the specific location; is it in one place all the time or does it move or radiate to other parts of the body? Perhaps it's a sharp pain behind your eye that changes to tension spreading across the back of your head and then into both shoulders.

Once you've identified the physical area, start by giving it some mental attention. Sit still and breathe into it, concentrating your breathing into the point of the tension or pain and releasing the tension on the out breath. Ask yourself, 'What feeling is associated with this pain?' and then wait. Don't try to guess; your *body* needs to tell you – not your mind; you literally have to *feel* it first. When you do feel it, you may want to shout or cry, as this is a critical part of the releasing. To this end, it's a good idea doing this in a safe and relatively insulated environment!

Practice this before going to sleep or at a break in your day. Be aware that it took time to build the armour, and it will also take time to dissolve it. Little by little, you'll start to experience the lightness of having cast off – or at least loosened – your emotional armour, and be rewarded with a lighter step through life, a more optimistic disposition and closer relationship with the present moment.

Freedom Phrase: 'To escape fear you have to go *through* it – not around'

Also see: Feel It – page 64

And try this practice: Vocal Cleansing – page 105

See the Everyday Gurus.

'Everyday, unassuming gurus show up in our space,
offering life lessons that can help us get over our shortcomings.'
Rob White, Author, Storyteller & Philosopher

The word 'guru' is often used to denote someone who has devoted his or her life to obtaining an enlightened state of being, or someone who has attained an extraordinarily high level of understanding about life. It's easy to believe that people like that have walked a different path from the rest us, and sacrificed much to obtain insights on how best to live. They may also be given labels such as *saint, mentor* or *guide* and are treated with respect and benevolence. They are seen as special. Sacred. Separate from us.

Yet, rather than having enlightenment bestowed upon us by a higher power, many of our pivotal life lessons are derived from far less grandiose sources, from ordinary people and circumstances as we go about our daily life. Whilst we don't always heed these lessons, they are presented to us nonetheless, keenly awaiting our readiness to clear the mental clutter in order to receive them.

Right now your life is full of *everyday gurus*: teachers who come disguised as regular (and occasionally, rather annoying), people. They might try to help you, or they may not. Perhaps they won't even notice you…but you'll notice them. And from this seemingly innocuous encounter, a new insight – or even a significant breakthrough – can be gained. But you must firstly be open to it.

From a playful child, you are reminded of how important it is to live lightly and free from inhibitions. From a handicapped person riding the bus, you may have cause to ponder the human qualities of determination and perseverance. You may even see your *own* flaws reflected in the eyes of parents angrily scolding their child, prompting you to act with more compassion and care with the people in your life.

In order to receive these lessons, you must be willing to suspend your own flurry of inner dialogue and judgement, surrender to your environment, and observe with curiosity and compassion. You can then watch the dance of life going on around you, and appreciate its beauty and humour. The most evolved amongst us tend to share this one great quality; they find the folly of everyday life *very* amusing. When you find yourself smiling as you receive a life lesson from a complete stranger – take it as a sign you're on the right track!

The American billionaire industrialist Andrew Carnegie once said he encountered someone *nearly every day* who offered him a valuable learning experience. This was a man who was revered for his business acumen, his wealth and status, yet he held dear the simple notion that we are all here to learn from each other, and that everyone has a nugget of gold for us, if we are just open to receiving it.

Using curiosity as your guide, try to look at the world as it *is* – not as it *should be*. Notice the small things, the moment of connection that you'd otherwise overlook in your rush towards your destination e.g. the warmth and authenticity of two friends chatting, the intensity of a businessman doing a phone deal, the wide inquisitive eyes of a toddler staring right at you. *These* are the things to be appreciated, even treasured. *This* is life – in high definition and 3D – and you're incredibly fortunate to be here to experience it all unfold.

As you move through the next few days, weeks and months, try slowing down just a little and take pause to look and listen a bit more intently at what is going on around you. Keep alert and aware (by avoiding getting lost in mind-time) and you will start to see all manner of wonderful things taking place: people just like you, doing their best to get by and make a difference in their own small way. Open yourself up to connecting with them from a place of presence and peace, and you may just find the solution to a problem, that you've been grappling with, comes to you from the most surprising and unexpected source.

Freedom Phrase: 'People are either a *blessing* or a *lesson*.'

Also see: Look for the Like – page 62

And try this practice: Notice the Moment – page 83

PART IV:

PRESENT PRACTICES

Practice Guide.

While being present is one of the easiest and most natural things for us to do, because we are away in our thoughts so much, we tend to be focused on either on the past or the future, and not the moment we are in.

In this section of the book, you will find a series of practical ideas to help guide you out of Mind-time and back into the here and now. They are called 'Practices' because they take *practice* in order for them to become habits. The practices themselves are very straightforward – it's finding the discipline to apply them that takes all the effort!

As you read through this section, take note of the practices that make you smile or that trigger a memory, and then try them out at the earliest possible opportunity. You may also want to use them in different combinations – there are no hard and fast rules here. You may even be inclined to make up your own present practices based on these ideas. Go for it.

The focus of this section is to provide you with simple guidelines that you can use as needed to help bring your attention back into the moment.

There are 18 Present Practices divided into three broad categories:

1. **Maintenance**: Practices that may be applied throughout your day for a consistent (re)connection to the moment (page 79).
2. **Corrective**: Course-correcting practices that help get you back on track (page 93).
3. **In Case of Emergency**: Reframing practices to help you deal with intense emotions and trying times (page 107).

Happy travelling!

MAINTENANCE PRACTICES

1. Just Breathe
2. Notice the Moment
3. Rush of Appreciation
4. Sit Straight, Walk Tall
5. Line up, Cool down
6. Follow Your Bliss

Just Breathe.

'If you want to conquer the anxiety of life, live in the moment, live in the breath.'
Amit Ray, Spiritual Master, Former Scientist

Why this practice?

Many of us have a tendency towards shallow breathing - this is because so much time is invested into thinking (or worrying). Shallow breathing interrupts our body's natural deep breathing cycle, leading to less oxygen being present in the bloodstream and an accumulation of tension in the body.

The simple process of regularly taking the time to practice diaphragmatic breathing will help you to simultaneously relax your body and mind. With continued practice, you will find that your energy levels will improve and your mind will become sharper.

Try this practice when:

- You've just finished a period of intensive thinking.
- You feel tension in your back, neck and shoulders.
- You have tightness or burning sensation in your tummy.

Setting yourself up:

- Find a comfortable chair or spot.
- If possible, remove yourself from technology and distractions.

Simply follow these steps:

- Place one hand on your chest and the other just below your ribcage and breathe normally.
- Notice which hand rises and falls the most; if the hand on your chest is rising more than the one on your abdomen, then you are shallow breathing.
- Now take a deep breath through your nose into your belly and watch your hand there rise (note that the hand on your chest should hardly move).
- Breathe into your belly again and count slowly to the count of 5 and hold the breath for a second at number '6'.

- Breathe out through your mouth by pursing your lips (like you're blowing through a straw) and continue the count until 10 or more.
- Repeat this process 5 or more times or until you are feeling more centred and relaxed.

Further notes & considerations:

- Diaphragmatic breathing is known to activate the vagus nerve (see page 11), which slows the heart rate and clears the mind–body connection.
- It can help to picture the diaphragm, which is a sheet of internal skeletal muscle that extends across the bottom of the rib cage, separating the chest cavity from the abdominal cavity.
- As the diaphragm contracts, the volume of the chest cavity increases, and air is drawn into the lungs.
- An added bonus is that breathing into the diaphragm also helps to massage the abdominal organs and improve digestive functioning.

Notice the Moment.

'You must live in the present, launch yourself on every wave, find your eternity in each moment.'
Henry David Thoreau, Author, Poet, Transcendentalist

Why this practice?

With so much of our attention projected forward into future possibilities, or backwards on past events, it's easy to find ourselves in a present moment that is left wanting or that somehow feels insufficient.

This practice helps to cut through the dense layer of thought that we carry into the moment with us. It helps us stay grounded in what *is*, rather than how we perceive things should (or could) be.

Try this practice when:

- You are stuck in Mind-time (worrying, figuring, planning, etc.).
- You are on the way to work or on the way home.
- You are at the grocery store.
- You are sitting in traffic.

Setting yourself up:

- Remind yourself that quality of life arises from being in tune with the world.
- Make a commitment to catch yourself overthinking and try this practice.

Simply follow these steps:

- Ask yourself: 'Will thinking about this *right now* help me to resolve this problem or issue?'
- If the answer is *no*, then loosen your grip on the thought by refocusing your attention back on your immediate environment.
- Notice the subtle elements of life that surround you, perhaps the
  o Colour of the trees outside the window reflecting the afternoon light
  o Sound of kids playing at the local school
  o Smell of home cooking
  o Feel of soft sheets or comfy cushions
  o Taste of fresh fruit

- o   Sadness in someone's eyes
  - Sit with these for a moment and appreciate the time you've allowed yourself to connect with what is real – with what *is*.

Further notes & considerations:

- Be prepared for your mind to fight for the right to keep mulling over the thoughts – after all, it's likely you haven't stopped them much in the past.
- It's the little things that are important for this exercise, things that typically get overlooked. Try looking through the eyes of a child again – be curious.
- At the end of the day, once again reflect on what you've noticed. Bring the feeling of calm you experienced into the moment you are now in.

Rush of Appreciation (ROA).

'Dwell on the beauty of life. Watch the stars, and see yourself running with them.'
Marcus Aurelius, Roman Emperor, Philosopher King

Why this practice?

Sometimes, when our minds are focused on what we want in the future, it's easy to miss the amazing things that already exist in our present. Instead of noticing and appreciating these, we often step over them as we look for something else to be happy or thankful for.

The Rush of Appreciation (ROA) takes things around you that you usually take for granted, and turns them into objects of wonder and appreciation. By regularly flexing your *appreciation muscle*, you will find yourself feeling more centred and connected to the situation you are in.

Try this practice when:

- You already feel relatively good and want to feel even better.
- You are driving between appointments or riding the bus.
- You are sitting outside on a bench having lunch.

Setting yourself up:

- No real set-up is required for this practice – just a gentle reminder to yourself to stop and smell the roses.

Simply follow these steps:

- Notice when your mind is operating in *future mode*.
- Call your attention to your immediate environment – what do you see?
- Look for things that you would usually overlook: the neatness of newly mowed lawns, the smooth and well-marked road or the well-constructed chair you are sitting on.
- Identify as many things as possible to appreciate in a 3 to 5-minute window – it's amazing what you can find to appreciate!

THE PRESENT.

Example:

- This is a very smooth road.
- They've done a great job on marking those white lines.
- They must have worked hard to build such a nice road.
- It's great that I can use this road to comfortably get to my destination.

Or perhaps:

- This car is great.
- Even though it's raining, I'm still dry.
- I'm so lucky to be able to move at speed through this and stay conformable.
- It's incredible how little energy is required to make this car move.
- It's amazing what people are capable of building…get it?

Further notes & considerations:

- It's tempting for us to always be looking at what's *wrong* with things and/or people – and this separation (seeing ourselves as separate or better) is one of the major causes of pain and disharmony. The ROA helps us to reverse this habit and look for things that are admirable in order to heal and create unity.
- You'll be amazed at how, once you switch on the ROA, not only do you start to feel relaxed and centred, but also things look brighter, people smile more – and you begin to attract more of that which you appreciate.

Sit Straight, Walk Tall.

'Never slouch, as doing so compresses the lungs, overcrowds other vital organs,
rounds the back and throws you off balance.'
Joseph H Pilates, Founder of Pilates

Why this practice?

Many of us spend more than half our waking hours sitting down either in the car, on the bus, having lunch, and of course, at a desk. Cramps develop in our necks and shoulders, but these are ignored because our minds are off elsewhere, leaving our bodies to suffer in silence.

When we do get a chance to get up and walk around, we are rarely aware of our posture or breathing, as our attention is still stuck in our thoughts and not in the here and now. This practice prompts you to bring your attention back to your body so that you keep sharp and centred.

Try this practice when:

- You notice tension building in your head, neck, back or shoulders.
- You have emerged from a period of deep concentration or daydreaming.
- Your mind is 'flighty' and keeps drifting off into random thought.

Setting yourself up:

- Remind yourself that you perform best when your body and mind are in tune.
- Make a decision to regularly refocus your attention on your body, which also bring you into the present.

Simply follow these steps:

When sitting:

- Push your bottom back into the chair, sit up straight and feel your solar plexus expand.
- Gently roll your shoulders and neck to bring consciousness and feeling back to them.
- Take three deep breaths into your belly and exhale slowly.

THE PRESENT.

When walking:

- Become aware of your posture and gait.
- Elongate your spine and open up your chest as you walk.
- Breathe from the belly into your solar plexus region, and tune your breathing to the rhythm of your walk.

Further notes & considerations:

- Bring your attention to your body at least a few times each day.
- This practice is just as important on days off as it is at work, so try to make it a 7-day-a-week practice.
- The more you become aware of your stance and posture throughout each day, the more likely you are to correct it and therefore avoid tension headaches and surprise (and costly) strains, pulled muscles and other injuries.

Line up, Cool down.

*'You have to imagine a waiting that is not impatient
because it is timeless.'*
R.S. Thomas, Poet, Author, Wales Enthusiast

Why this practice?

It's a common mindset that queuing or waiting too long for anything is at best undesirable and at worst *unbearable*. You may even start to believe that there is some malicious force at work behind the scenes, disrupting the flow of your life and making you run late.

But instead of viewing the wait time as *wasted*, what if you were to use it a chance to refresh and renew? After all, life can be busy enough without adding more needless worry and stress to it.

Try this practice when:

- You find yourself frustrated by having to wait.
- You've been rushing around.
- You're waiting at traffic lights, the departure lounge, the bank, etc.

Setting yourself up:

- Start seeing time to queue as a welcomed break.
- Remember to put your state of being first (Shield Your State).

Simply follow these steps:

- When waiting in line, tell yourself something like, 'Great, time to practice being present!'
- Straighten your spine and take a deep breath.
- Count your breaths to 10 (you can use the Just Breathe practice from page 81).
- Pass a friendly glance or smile at the person next to you. Your presence may also help them.
- Notice how you feel when you finally get served: Calmer? More alert?

Further notes & considerations:

- The more you practice this, the easier and more effective it becomes.

- We're all *conditioned* to feel frustrated when waiting for things, so it may take a few runs at it for you to relax enough to enjoy the wait.
- If you're feeling angry or particularly frustrated, it's even more important to use this valuable time to find your centre.

Follow Your Bliss.

'Follow your bliss and don't be afraid,
and doors will open where you didn't know they were going to be.'
Joseph Campbell, Writer, Mythologist, Track & Field Star

Why this practice?

In a in busy world, it's easy to get distracted by your thoughts and get yourself all wound up. But there are no doubt certain activities that you love to partake in, and that bring you into the moment without you even trying. These activities could be called 'hobbies' or 'play' – but they also count as *practices*.

These are your *bliss* activities; and they are also the best and easiest ways for you to get a direct connection to the present.

Try this practice when:

- You've been very busy at work.
- You've been concentrating intensively for some time.
- You feel restless or frustrated.

Setting yourself up:

- Notice yourself getting pulled into the mindset of being 'too busy' or 'not having enough time', etc.

Simply follow these steps:

Make a list (mental or written) of the things that you enjoy spending time doing. This will be your bliss list, and might include thing like:

- Playing with your kids, nieces, nephews, etc.
- Singing in the shower or car
- Playing musical instruments
- Surfing, skiing, etc.
- Laughing with friends
- Holding your loved one
- Listening to your favourite song or type of music

- Walking through nature
- Sitting in the sun

Now, try to implement one or more of these activities *every day* – or as often as possible, and build it into your routine.

Example:

- In the morning, you listen to your favourite song as you make breakfast.
- At lunch, you sit out in the sun and call your loved one.
- In the afternoon, you share a laugh with your friends or co-workers.
- In the evening, you cook (or enjoy) a lovely meal.
- At night, you have a bath, cuddle you kids/loved one/teddy bear…etc.

Further notes & considerations:

- Your 'bliss' activities are things that you *already* have in your life. The key is to incorporate them as part of your daily medicine for a happier and more balanced life.
- You may feel like you're slacking off, but this is something you're doing in order to keep YOU healthy and productive. Soon you'll find that you won't need to make excuses for it – it simply becomes too important.

CORRECTIVE PRACTICES

1. Be in the Conversation
2. Gratitude List
3. Empowering Affirmations
4. Come to Your Senses
5. Body Scan
6. Vocal Cleansing

Be in the Conversation.

'The only reason why we ask other people how their weekend was
is so we can tell them about our own weekend.'
Chuck Palahniuk, Author of *Invisible Monsters*

Why this practice?

Often, when in conversations with others, our minds are in a constant flux of thought, labelling and comparing what they say (or how they look) to what we consider to be correct or normal. This mode of interaction keeps at least some of our focus directed out of the moment and limiting the potential within the interaction.

This practice is about becoming more aware of your wandering mind when conversing with others, and reigning in it so you can be more present in your interactions – which helps others to become more so as well.

Try this practice when:

- You notice your mind wandering or tuning out of a conversation.
- You are impatient and want to get your point across.
- You feel like you've got something more important to do.
- You want to improve your interactions with important people in your life.

Setting yourself up:

- Make a commitment to yourself to become more aware of the thoughts flashing through your mind when interacting with others.
- See this approach as a way of improving the quality of your relationships with others.

Simply follow these steps:

- As you start a conversation, make a conscious decision to clear your mind of the any assumptions or preconceived notions you may be carrying with you – to clear the slate.
- Redirect your focus onto the person you are speaking to and
  - Listen with *your ears*: Hear their tone of voice and use of language – but try not to judge.
  - Listen with *your eyes*: Look into their eyes as they are speaking and notice their facial expressions and manner – again try not to judge.

  o Listen with *your body*: Notice any feelings you may have; what is your gut telling you?
- When you find your mind wandering, refocus your attention on what you're hearing, seeing and sensing.
- Try not to interrupt them, and then wait for a second or two before responding.
- Trust yourself enough to reply spontaneously – this is the *real you* they want to connect with.

Further notes & considerations:

- At first, this practice may be extremely difficult, as your mind is so quick to analyse others and make judgments.
- If it helps, take a breath to centre yourself.
- Be gentle on yourself, you are trying to undo a lifetime of habits. Give it time.

Gratitude List.

Why this practice?

In our consumerist culture, it's easy for you to get fixated on your next purchase or experience (be it a new car, new house or holiday) and take for granted all the wonderful things that *already exist* in your life.

This simple practice serves to remind you of the riches you already have at your feet, not only making you feel better about your current life situation, but also encouraging more good things to come your way.

Try this practice when:

- You want to deepen your appreciation of life.
- You feel like your current situation is incomplete.
- You're feeling jealous or sorry for yourself.
- You *don't* feel grateful.

Setting yourself up:

- Grab some nice paper and a pen.
- Find a relaxing position, on the couch, in a comfortable chair or even in bed.

Simply follow these steps:

- Find a moment of repose, take a deep breath and be still.
- Start bringing things to mind that you are thankful for (they could be as simple as a comfy pillow, a healthy child or an affectionate cat).
- Note them down in no particular order.
- Stick this list where you will see it daily, like your bathroom mirror or on the back of your car visor.
- Make a point of acknowledging the content of the list at least daily – or until you're feeling more connected and thankful again.

Further notes & considerations:

- Even when you're not looking at your list, try to think of the main things as often as possible – feeling lucky often creates luck!
- When you feel like you're *not* getting what you want, try using this line: 'I'm looking forward to having (*insert wonderful thing*) in the future – but right now I am so thrilled I have (*insert gems at your feet*).' Straight away, you'll be back in the moment while simultaneously drawing what you want closer.
- A great time to employ this practice is when you've just gone to bed. Start with how grateful you are for your comfy bed, and go from there…

Empowering Affirmations.

Why this practice?

It's unfortunate that, for one reason or another, many of us succumb to negative thinking about either ourselves or others at times. It may come as a result of childhood conditioning, poor role models or perhaps being influenced a media that plays to our insecurities.

If we're not careful, negative (or overly sceptical) thinking can become our default thinking, which only creates more problems. Life-affirming thoughts can help to rebalance the scales, help us to feel stronger, and rise above the issues.

Try this practice when:

- You notice you are putting yourself down.
- You find yourself judging or criticising others.
- You feel ill at ease in your surroundings.

Setting yourself up:

- Clear some mental space.
- Make a *decision* to turn the tide of your thinking.

Simply follow these steps:

- Notice any negative thoughts you may be carrying about yourself or others.
- Recognise that these thoughts do nothing to help anyone – in fact, they can often hurt.
- Identify a positive affirmation that flips your thinking, and use it to replace the negative thought.
- Repeat the affirmation to yourself whenever the negative thought arises.
- Use this new thought as a guide for your actions.

Examples to try:

- When you are unsure or anxious about a decision: 'My wisdom will guide me to the best decision.'

- When you are insecure or lonely: 'I love and approve of myself.'
- When you are nervous around strangers: 'I am beautiful and smart, and that's how everybody sees me'.
- When you don't want to face the day: 'Today will be a gorgeous day to remember'.

Further notes & considerations:

- Negative thinking takes root through repetition – and so will your positive thoughts.
- If you are you are able to, say the affirmation out aloud, as this adds more power to the practice.
- If you feel silly, that's okay; old habits die hard, and the more resistance you experience, the more worthwhile the work is.
- Feel free to come up with your own affirmation; the only rule is that is has to be positive, empowering and must make you feel something when you think or say it.

Come to Your Senses.

'Lose your mind and come to your senses.'
Frederick Salomon Perls, Psychotherapist, Father of 'Gestalt' Therapy

Why this practice?

When you're stuck in Mind-time, your attention is internal and not focused on your immediate environment. This causes you to lose touch with what is going on around you, affecting your ability to respond effectively to situations you encounter and causing you to lose touch with your feelings.

Coming to your *senses* is one of the most direct ways to connect with the world around you, as your senses pick up what is happening in this moment: how things look, feel, sound, smell and taste right now (this is why you enjoy nice meals so much!)

Try this practice when:

- You've been deep in thought on a project or matter.
- You are doing routine tasks such as showering, cooking, chores, etc.
- You're walking out for coffee or lunch.

Setting yourself up:

- Think about your preferred sense – do you prefer to watch, listen, smell or touch?

Simply follow these steps:

- Focus your preferred sense on something in your environment.
- Just *notice* what you sense; don't label it 'good' or 'bad'.
- Go deeper into it; concentrate your attention on it.
- Open up to your other senses – what else do you notice?
- Accept all of it *just as it is* and remind yourself that you are lucky to be alive to appreciate this.

Example:

You're having a shower...

- Notice the feeling of the warm water running down your back.
- Notice the scent of your soap.
- Feel the texture of your hair or skin.
- Notice the steam rising and how it is extracted or collects on the shower door.
- Reach out and draw a smiley face…

Further notes & considerations:

- It's likely you are already doing this practice to some extent – so just gear it up further.
- You can practice this in your seat by simply noticing the weight of your body/bum on the chair – or by noticing the tingling of energy in your hands.
- Of all your senses, your most direct experience of life is how you feel *inside*, so tune into this regularly and breathe through any discomfort.

Body Scan.

Why this practice?

Taking time out to still your mind with meditation is known to be beneficial to both your physical and mental health, yet many people find meditation to be just too big a leap for them to take from where they are at right now.

The body scan practice is widely used in yoga as it helps to relax the body and remove tension that is being held onto. The secret to its popularity is that, rather than asking you to *turn off* your thoughts, it requires you to *focus* and utilise them as part of the practice.

Try this practice when:

- You have trouble getting to sleep.
- You feel overly restless or anxious.
- You notice your breathing is shallow.

Setting yourself up:

- Remove yourself from distractions.
- Sit comfortably, or if you can, lie down.
- Turn your phone off or switch it to silent mode (not vibrate).

Simply follow these steps:

- Narrow your attention to one area in the body.
- Hold your attention there for a few moments.
- See the area in your mind's eye; feel the energy flowing through it.
- Gently move your attention to the neighbouring area, once again pausing just for a moment to experience it.
- Continue up your body, pausing at as many intervals as you like.

THE PRESENT.

Example:

- Lying down comfortably, you bring your attention to your small toe.
- You notice the warmth in it, and see it in your mind's eye.
- You move onto the next toe, and the next one and across to the heel; soon you are feeling your entire foot.
- You work up to the ankle, the calf, the knee, the hip.
- Soon you feel your whole leg: alive, warm, present.
- Then move onto the next leg and eventually up your torso to your face and head.

Further notes & considerations:

- You may just scan one area, for example, your fingers and hand, or your whole body.
- For a whole body scan, it's best to start at your feet and work upwards.
- When you open your eyes, try to stay still for a moment to appreciate the balance of your internal feeling with the outside world.

Vocal Cleansing.

'Do you know that our soul is composed of harmony?'
Leonardo da Vinci, Painter, Sculptor, Mathematician, Vegetarian

Why this practice?

In a world where we have to be careful about what we say, to whom we say it, and the manner in which things are said, it's easy for us to feel like we've *lost our voice*, or to perhaps feel that what we have to say is it not valid or important.

Your brain acts as the gatekeeper for your mouth, and it will stop you (often for good reason) from expressing a thought (or sound) it believes will make you look bad or silly. When this happens repeatedly, energy builds up around the throat and jaw, which can lead to sore throats – even speech impediments.

This practice gives you permission to express yourself through the vibration of your voice, thereby clearing the channel and bringing you back into a better harmony with yourself.

Try this practice when:

- Your throat feels constricted.
- You feel pressure or constriction in your solar plexus.
- You're trying to relax after a hard day.
- You feel you haven't been able to express yourself.
- Before going to sleep.

Setting yourself up:

- Find a space away from others. It could be your shower of bath or, if you are outside your home, your car is ideal.
- Be prepared to feel a little bit silly at first – and be okay with that.

Simply follow these steps:

- Sit or stand straight with your back lengthened.
- Take a deep belly breath, and as you breathe out, make a descending *'ahhhh'* sound for at least 5 seconds.

- Start the '*ahhhh*' sound from the top of your throat and let it travel down to your body as it continues.
- Repeat it again and feel the vibration through your chest and solar plexus.
- Continue until you feel a warm glow of energy within your body.

Further notes & considerations:

- The '*ahhhh*' sounds is similar to the sound you might make after having a very tasty meal (a satisfied sound).
- The '*ahhhh*' sound is well known to be a healing sound and promotes wellbeing.
- Try placing two fingers on your solar plexus, and you will feel the vibration of your chest cavity – this can help you further enhance the practice.

I.C.O.E PRACTICES
(IN CASE OF EMERGENCY)

1. Control the Controllable
2. Let it Go
3. Change the Script
4. Counting Breaths
5. Me-Time
6. Digital Detox

Control the Controllable.

'God grant me the serenity to accept the things I cannot change,
the courage to change the things I can, and the wisdom to know the difference.'
The Serenity Prayer, widely used in 12-Step programs

Why this practice?

It's tempting to blame others for the difficulties we experience; your boss for working you too hard, your friend or partner for turning up late, or half the city for the heavy traffic on the freeway! While it's easy to hold others accountable for your situation, in the end it often leads down a path of frustration and separation.

The keys to maintaining your composure is to be able to differentiate that which is *within* your control versus that which is *outside* of it. Getting upset about people, things or situations beyond your control is nonsensical, and leaves you feeling emotionally drained. Taking action in those situations that are within your control however will empower you and bring you into the moment.

Try this practice when:

- You feel aggrieved or wronged by someone.
- You are feeling angry or frustrated with the situation you are in.
- You find yourself saying and doing things that are making the situation worse rather than better.

Setting yourself up:

- Step back from the situation (even if it's just in your head).
- Be willing to suspend your judgment and blame for a while.

Simply follow these steps:

- Clarify the issue that is bothering you.
- Ask yourself, 'Is this situation (or feeling) within my control?'
- If the answer is *yes*, then be courageous enough to take the action you feel is most appropriate.
- If the answer is *no* then you must find a way to accept the situation as it stands.
- By accepting what you cannot control, you free up energy and resources that are better applied to those things you can.

THE PRESENT.

Example: You are running late to an engagement but there is heavy traffic on the highway.

You can control (and therefore can take action on):

- Tuning into the traffic report on the local radio to hear of any alternative routes that may be available.
- Safely manoeuvring through traffic to the lanes moving more quickly.
- Calling ahead to inform you companion that you may be running a little late.

You cannot control (and therefore must accept):

- The traffic slowing down – or coming to a standstill.
- The exact time you may eventually arrive at your engagement.

Further notes & considerations:

- Accepting that there is no action you can take at that moment does not mean there is no action to take in the future. These situations are best viewed as a learning experienced that will avoid you repeating the situation at a later time.
- Commit to exercising control where you have it, and to let go of the notion that you have power over situations where in fact you do not.

Let It Go.

Why this practice?

One of the hardest things we have to do as human beings is let go of things that we have become attached to, be it a possession, a feeling, or in some cases, a relationship. The simple act of letting go evokes primal fears in us: fears of loss, rejection and uncertainty.

We can only carry so much through our lives before it overburdens us – and *letting go* means gaining the ability to live more lightly.

Try this practice when:

- You are worrying excessively over some issue.
- You feel hurt or wronged.
- Your cause pain or hurt to others through your anger or emotions.
- You realise that you're clinging to something that needs to be let go of.

Setting yourself up:

- Make some time for yourself.
- Release some of the hurt or frustration by crying or yelling out aloud if necessary.
- Remind yourself that your *state of being* is the most important thing for you to nurture and protect.

Simply follow these steps:

- Clarify the thought or issue that is weighing so heavily on you.
- Ask yourself, 'Is there any action I can take now to resolve this?'
- If there is, then *take the action necessary to resolve the issue.*
- If there's no action to take, make a conscious choice to let it go (at least for now).
- To let it go, you might try:
  - The Just Breathe or Vocal Cleansing practice
  - Sharing with others
  - Minimising the issue by comparing it to others who may be far less fortunate that you.

- Create some space by enjoying a well-loved activity (Follow Your Bliss)
- Practicing an affirmation such as, 'When I let go, my soul thanks me.'
- Having a laugh with friends or seeing a comedy show.

Further notes & considerations:

- Remember that you *always* have an option to let things go – *nothing* is worth holding onto to the point that it causes you or others to suffer needlessly.
- It takes more effort to hold on than to let go and by making letting so a habit, you will find yourself with more energy and vitality.

Change the Script.

Why this practice?

When you are upset, you're usually driven by the negative thoughts in your life and not the positive ones. The feelings of unhappiness can be so intense that they can cause physical pain: in your chest, neck or back – even migraines.

These symptoms can be the product of an emotional charge that has been generated by an idea (or story) you have repeating to yourself – a script that you have written and an inner dialogue running 24/7. As long as you keep telling yourself the same story, any feeling of *dis*-ease will persist. To change the feeling, you must first change the script.

Try this practice when:

- You feel aggrieved or deeply upset.
- You feel unable to let go of something that has been said or done to you.
- You are in danger of hurting others through words or actions.

Setting yourself up:

- Remove yourself from the source of the frustration.
- Go for a walk or a drive.
- Avoid direct contact with people until you have calmed your emotions.

Simply follow these steps:

- Clarify the *predominate* thought or idea that is upsetting you. Bring it into words.
- Remind yourself that this is only *one* way of looking at the situation – there are other scripts available to you. They can make you feel stronger.
- Think of someone you greatly admire for their wisdom and perspective on life; how would *they* view the very same situation?

- Create a bridge from the hurtful thought to a less hurtful one, and then to one that is empowering (or has less of a sting).
- Turn your attention to a thought that makes you feel more empowered.

Example:

- Hurtful thought: 'He made me feel like an idiot. How *dare* he!'
- Less hurtful thought: 'I can see it from his perspective, but I didn't deserve *that* response.'
- Empowering thought: 'That outburst was unusual…perhaps he's having a bad day…I should check what's going on with him.'

Further notes & considerations:

- Your quality of life is largely determined by your inner equilibrium, so you must do what you can to shield your state.
- Your most reliable indicator of whether your thoughts are serving you or not are your emotions – take heed of them.
- When you do feel emotionally distraught, it is a sure sign that you need to change the script!

Counting Breaths.

'No food or drug will ever do for you what a fresh supply of oxygen will.'
Tony Robbins, Motivational Speaker, Life Coach, NLP Advocate

Why this practice?

To breathe is such a natural part of our life that we tend to take it for granted, not noticing how shallow it becomes when we are unwittingly and compulsively chasing after our thoughts.

This practice will help you to slow your mind by tuning into and controlling your breathing. It's not exactly meditation, but it's close. Once you are able to tune into your breath, you will find yourself more relaxed, centred and present.

Try this practice when:

- You have trouble getting to sleep.
- You can't seem to stop thinking about something.
- You feel stressed out or overwhelmed with worry.

Setting yourself up:

- Remove yourself from distractions.
- Sit comfortably, or if you can, lie down.
- Turn the phone off or switch it to silent mode (not vibrate).

Simply follow these steps:

- Start by counting each breath and see how high you can go *without drifting off into thought*.
- Each time you drift off and lose count, start back at 'one' again.
- Don't be too hard on yourself; if you lose track, simply start over.

Example:

- *(Take the first breath and start counting)* '1…2…3…4…5…'
- *(Thought appears)* 'I wonder how high I can get to?'
- *(Restart count)* '1…2…3…4…5…6…7…8'
- *(Thought appears)* 'I can't believe she said that to me…'
- *(Restart count)* '1…2…3…4…5…6…7…8…9…10…'
- *Etc.*

Further notes & considerations:

- Every full breath (both in and out) counts as 'one'.
- Don't scold yourself for thinking; instead, just notice the thought (and perhaps smile to yourself) and then start back at one.
- If your thoughts are particularly intense, try extending your count to 30, 50 or even 100 or more.
- Soon you'll find yourself entering a relaxed state and loosening the grip your thoughts have on you.

For more on this and other practices, go to www.thepresentbook.com.au/practices.

Me-Time.

Why this practice?

When's the last time you spent more than 24 hours alone, with only yourself for company? How about 2 hours? 10mins?

Whilst some may wish for less alone time (in which case this practice may not apply), others are so busy running between different places (family to work to friends and back to family again) that they neglect make time to allow themselves to get recharged. This is a particularly common state for working parents.

Me-time is simply about creating a window in which to savour some precious time alone. It doesn't matter so much *what* you are doing – or even how long you are doing it for – it's far more about how you are *feeling* when you do it.

Try this practice when:

- You feel as if you've been facing a never-ending stream of challenges.
- You are getting snappy or short with those you love.
- You feel like your daily life has become less important or meaningful.
- You feel like you're being pulled in too many directions.
- You feel emotionally or physically drained.

Setting yourself up:

- Remind yourself that you cannot serve others fully unless you are 'topped up' yourself.
- Make a commitment to prioritise your *own* needs – and not just those of others.

Simply follow these steps:

- Check your schedule; find an open spot in the near future.
- If there is no open slot, *create one* by delegating tasks to others or postponing events.
- Fill the next available gap with the words: me-time!
- Plan your favourite activity, something that makes you feel nurtured and happy. Examples could include getting a massage, reading a book by the sea, going for a bike ride or listening to your favourite music while having a soak.

Further notes & considerations:

- While this practice sounds very easy to do, you must ask yourself, 'Am I *actually* doing it?' If not, why not?
- Some people with responsibilities may feel guilty that they are shirking responsibilities, but the opposite is true.
- If you *must* justify your me-time, simply count this activity as part of your mental health exercise program!

Digital Detox.

'The devices meant to simplify our lives merely create new and improved complexities.'
Susan Maushart, author of *The Winter of Our Disconnect*

Why this practice?

Of all the things that busy our minds throughout the day, it's our increasing reliance on – and addiction to – personal technology that pushes us towards our terminal thinking velocity. If we're not working at a computer, we might be checking social media on the phone, watching TV or playing video games. It seems there are so many distractions and so little time!

Switching devices to the *off* position for a period of time might not seem like a hard thing to do – but how often is it done? Instead, devices are commonly read and played in bed, churning up even more thoughts, well after the body is ready to retire for the day.

Try this practice when:

- You notice yourself checking emails or social media incessantly.
- You feel restless and your usual relaxation habits are not helping.
- You are trying to relax after a hard day.
- You want to share quality time with friends and family.

Setting yourself up:

- Choose a time (or day) where you're not expecting any important communication.
- Throw out a challenge to yourself (and perhaps others) to go 'tech-free' for an agreed period of time.
- Tell yourself that *you* are the master of your technology – not the other way around.

Simply follow these steps:

- If necessary, let your family and friends know that you will be 'off the grid' for a time.
- Switch off your main devices (just putting them on silent or vibrate defeats the purpose).
- Whenever you find yourself thinking about turning things on or checking in, instead take a moment to pause and take a deep breath.

- When you turn everything on again – notice how little has changed and how easy it was to be away for a time.
- Start making it a habit.

Further notes & considerations:

- Remember, up until only recently, we were not 'dialled in' to the internet 24/7.
- Start by waiting an hour in the morning before turning on or checking your phone or email. See it as time to get your bearings for the day ahead.
- You could also dedicate one day a week or fortnight to being without your favourite tech toys (maybe a Sunday, for example) and instead devote this time to your partner or kids.

NOTES & INSPIRATIONS

The Next Step...

Thank you for taking the time to read this book.

It's my hope you have enjoyed the experience – and relished the concept – of becoming more present more often. But to really make a lasting positive change in your life (and in the lives of others), it takes more than just *having* the knowledge; it takes bringing it to life in your world through action.

The late, great, Stephen Covey Sr. (*of The Seven Habits of Highly Successful People fame*), perhaps said it best; 'To know and not to do, is to not really know at all!' How often have you listened to someone speak and thought to yourself, 'Yeah, I knew that'? It's very easy for us to delude ourselves into thinking that just knowing alone is enough. It is not.

To create a stronger connection to the moment (and to yourself) you must try *something new*, to take even one idea and test it out. It doesn't matter if you feel silly or uncomfortable - or even if you don't follow through with it. What's important is that you disrupt your pattern slightly.

The intention behind this book is to offer up a range of ideas, insights and practices to you that, with just small amount of effort, can become ingrained into your thinking and daily life. Start by focusing on the one idea of practice that really resonated with you; experiment with it, play with it, see how it fits you and what change it seeds within you. Even a one percent shift in behaviour can lead to a dramatically different outcome. Once you have aligned yourself with one principle or practice, try another – but only when it feels right.

When you start to experience the enormous benefits (and relief) of becoming more present – emotionally, mentally, physically – you may be tempted to try and convert others to your new way of thinking or feeling. There is no need to do this. Others will be positively affected by your new state without your saying or doing anything different. They may even ask you, 'What have you changed?', being aware that something is different, but not being able to put their finger on it. You will most benefit them by just being yourself, being open, being present.

I opened this book with a line from Marianne Williamson's beautiful poem 'Our Deepest Fear' and, as this book draws to a close, it seems fitting to return to the last line of her poem, *'As we are liberated from our own fear, our presence automatically liberates others.'* Shield your state and observe the incredibly positive impact you can make in your immediate world just by staying centred.

THE PRESENT.

There is no demand on you to change quickly, few people do. The only requirement is to slow down and start listening to your inner voice a little more often; the voice that says, 'Hey, steady on…stop worrying so much', a voice you so often ignore.

But perhaps most importantly of all, please try to keep in mind that this is all just a grand adventure – and you get the most out of it when you are able to let go and embrace the journey (and the lessons that come along with it). Your greatest asset is your ability to stay centred and present, both when alone and when around others. It will not only change you, it will literally change everything in your world.

Happy Travelling ~ Jason

'I am no more messiah than you. The river delights to lift us free, if only we dare let go.
Our true work is this voyage, this adventure.'
Richard Bach, *Illusions*

Book Inspirations

I will be eternally grateful to all the writers, speakers and enlightened thought leaders who have shared their insights so that I may soak in their wisdom and elevate my own being. Please continue your *Present* journey with this shortlist of wonderful books.

Book	Author	Why you need to read this book
Be Here Now	Baba Ram Dass	There is nothing quite like this book. It is a trip into the now with intricate illustrations accompanied with powerful quotes and insights.
Illusions	Richard Bach	A simple, beautiful book. It tells a fable with a powerful underlying message. Can be read quickly and contemplated slowly.
Jonathan Livingstone Seagull	Richard Bach	An absolute classic. Jonathan teaches us the power of mastery and breaking from the norm to feel fearless and free.
The Power of Now	Eckhart Tolle	Masterfully written and containing insight after insight, this must be one of the most important books on the subject in the past 50 years.
A New Earth	Eckhart Tolle	Going deeper into the *Power of Now*, Tolle put the larger concepts of presence into practical applications. Another must-read.
The Only Dance there Is	Baba Ram Dass	Transcribed from a lecture tour in the 1970s. Dass is eloquent, humorous and profound during the off-the-cuff talks he gives to his fans and followers.
Love – The Goal of Living	Rainer Taeni	A brilliant and comprehensive foray into the power of love and how it drives much of our lives.
To Have or to Be	Eric Fromm	In this academic masterpiece, Fromm provides an absorbing thesis on the difference between the two modalities of having and being.

Flow – The Science of Optimal Experience	Mihaly Csikszentmihalyi	The definitive book on the psychology of optimal experience, or 'Flow'. How to get present through consciously directed action.
Stillness is the Way	Barry Long	Transcribed from an intimate two-day intensive meditation retreat, Barry Long takes the reader, along with a handful of his students, on an insightful journey into the now.
The Happiness Hypothesis	Jonathan Haidt	A master thesis from a distinguished positive psychologist on the art and science of being happy.
Siddhartha	Herman Hesse	Written in the 1920s, the journey of Siddhartha is mystical but eminently relatable today. Siddhartha's is an adventure towards deep presence.
The Magicians Way	William Whitecloud	This tale follows the life of Mark Vale, as a group of contemporary alchemists teach him how to shift his perspective of time, space and personal power.
The Prophet	Kahlil Gibran	An incredibly poetic, reflective and heart-warming book. There are so many nuggets of gold that it must be read over multiple times.
Perfect Health	Deepak Chopra	A comprehensive manual on realigning your body, mind and spirit. Dr. Chopra balances western and eastern healing practices and points us towards the primary driver of perfect health – our inner state.

About the Author

Jason Jelicich was born in and raised in New Zealand. By the age of 10 he was selling newspapers on city street corners and by 12, he was helping with odd jobs around his father's hospitality business. Moving to Sydney in his late teens, Jason gained notoriety as an accomplished bartender and industry trainer before eventually establishing his own bartender training company.

Jason published his first book 'The Modern Bartender' in 2000, which helped to usher in a new era of professionalism and sophistication across the Australian drinks industry. Over the past 15 years, Jason has travelled the globe as a bar and restaurant consultant. His clients have included some of the world's top hospitality operators such as the Fontainebleau Resort in Miami and New York's Dead Rabbit, winner of Best Bar in the World 2016.

The purpose of his work continues to be creating healthy and profitable environments, where the people can connect, celebrate, and live in the moment.

Jason currently resides in Australia and is the proud father of Tyson, Hunter, Cormac & Elodie.

Enquiries and questions are welcome. Jason can be contacted via email at jasonjelicich@gmail.com

Printed in the United States
by Baker & Taylor Publisher Services